WHILE REASON SLEPT

THOMAS F. BRIER, JR.

ISBN-10: 1725982161
ISBN-13: 978-1725982161

To my best friends:
Mom, Dad, Jim and Matt

CONTENTS

ACKNOWLEDGMENTS

I derived an unexpected amount of enjoyment in writing this book. In many ways, it just wrote itself. But it would not have been possible without my family, who supported me every step of the way, and a few close friends—Tom Brown, Lorna Yzkanin, Shani Walker, and Maggie Sallusti—who generously donated their time to offer immensely helpful advice and feedback. To all of you, thank you for your encouragement and support throughout this process. It means more than you know.

PREFACE

"There is no greater evil one can suffer than to hate reasonable discourse."

Socrates

It was my Junior year in college that I first fell in love with philosophy. Or, more specifically, I suppose I first fell in love with thought experiments. You've no doubt heard of the Trolley Problem. A runaway train is barreling toward five innocents trapped on a train track. As chance would have it, you find yourself standing next to a lever that, if pulled, would redirect the train down a different track, thus saving five people from certain death. On the second track, however, is another person who is likewise incapable of escaping harm's way. Do you pull the lever, thereby killing the one person on the second track in order to save the five stranded on the first? Hmm.... I remember thinking. Yes, probably. The net gain is four lives saved. From a consequentialist standpoint, that seems to be the rational move.

But what if the one person on the second track is a family member? Well... In that scenario, I probably wouldn't pull the lever.

"Why?" you might ask. The outcome is no different; the net outcome of *not* pulling the lever would be four lives lost. Under your own logic then, TFB, you would be making an irrational decision.

That is true. But I could never kill a family member.

So, just to be clear, you're saying that your family member is more important than five other family members? How is that moral?

Well, I'm not really sure. Maybe I would pull the lever....

As a 20-year-old college student, my first encounter with the Trolley Problem went something along those lines. At this point, you may be thinking, when would one ever encounter such a moral dilemma in the real world? To that, I would ask you to consider the Blitz of Coventry.

During the second week of November in 1940—just a few weeks after FDR won election to a third term—Winston Churchill received a devastating report. At the time, Hitler had just celebrated a civilian bombing campaign unparalleled in human history. London was in ruins; thousands were dead.

The German bombing plans were, of course, coded. Occasionally, Britain was able to ascertain the location of a particular target by studying the *Knickebein* transmitter beams that guided the German bombers while in flight. These beams, however, generally weren't detectable until thirty minutes before the raiders took off. If the Brits were lucky, they could frantically activate their evacuation units, but such last-minute efforts usually weren't enough to save countless innocent civilians from death.

Thanks to remarkable progress made by codebreakers at Bletchley Park, however, the British Security Coordination (BSC) was able to intercept and decode Hitler's plan to destroy the English city of Coventry a mere minutes after Hitler issued the order. Armed with this advanced knowledge of the attack, Britain could warn families to immediately commence evacuation—a warning that could save thousands of lives.

But Churchill faced a dilemma. Bletchley—which at the time was unknown to the world save for Churchill and a few of his closest confidants—was making tremendous progress in penetrating the secret communications of the Axis Powers. Just a few days before Churchill received the Coventry report, Berlin had announced to the world a formal linkage with Rome and Tokyo. If Churchill issued an advanced evacuation notice, he would reveal to the enemy that he knew their plans. The immense value of Bletchley and its inestimable role in the ultimate fight for civilization would be lost.

Churchill opted against pulling the evacuation lever. Standard emergency protocols were kept in place. On the evening of November 14, 1940, Hitler launched 300 German bombers in a carnage crusade that killed or injured nearly 1,000 innocent people. The Germans deemed the raid so successful that they intended make every town in England "Coventryized" from that point forward.

Churchill was debilitated. Shortly after the Coventry raid, he met with William Stephenson—the head of BSC and arguably the most underrated genius of the past century. Churchill's anguish was palpable. "War is forcing us more and more to play God," he said. "I don't know what I should have done. . . ." As Stephenson would recall after the War, Churchill felt that he had aged "20 years" by letting Coventry burn.[1]

The Coventry Blitz is but one example of how seemingly fatuous moral dilemmas like the Trolley Problem can play out in real life. Others can be imagined as well. Currently perched on the event horizon is a world occupied by self-driving cars, a paradigm shift that promises to carry a host of new dilemmas. In a recent TED Talk, MIT professor and scientist Iyad Rahwan offered the following adaptation of the Trolley Problem to illustrate the questions we must address in deciding how we want our driverless cars to behave:

> Now picture yourself in a driverless car in the year 2030, sitting back and watching this vintage TEDxCambridge video. All of a sudden, the car experiences mechanical failure and is unable to stop. If the car continues, it will crash into a bunch of pedestrians crossing the street.
>
> But—the car may swerve, hitting one bystander, killing [the bystander] to save the pedestrians. What should the car do, and who should decide? What if instead the car could swerve into a wall, crashing and killing you, the passenger, in order to save those

pedestrians?[2]

From a consequentialist standpoint, it would seem rational to save as many people as possible, right? If so, then the car should either (a) hit the one bystander or (b) self-destruct, killing you, the driver. If the car chooses the former, should you be held legally responsible? And if the car chooses the latter, would you ever buy that car?

Other thought experiments are equally interesting. One of my favorites is the ship of Theseus. After a long battle, the celebrated ship sailed by the Greek hero Theseus docked at an Athenian harbor so the locals could get a first-hand view of history. Over time, though, the ship's wooden planks began to rot. To preserve its historical value, the locals decided to replace the old planks one-by-one with new planks until, after several decades, all of the original parts were gone. The ship, however, retained its natural form. This raises the question: Is the "restored" ship the same object as the "original" ship? If not, when did it change? After the swapping of the first plank, the last plank, or one of the planks in between? And if the ship *is* the same, then how can you account for the fact that its individual parts are different?

Applied today, the ship of Theseus problem is relevant to what many futurists call the "singularity." The singularity, in short, pertains to the intersection of human intelligence and artificial intelligence.

Renowned futurist and Director of Engineering at Google, Ray Kurzweil, predicts this will happen by 2045.[3*] So in Theseusian terms, if you connect your neocortex directly to the cloud—as Ray Kurzweil is intent on doing—is the data uploaded to the cloud still *your* mind? Or is it some sort of mind-machine hybrid? In other words, is it the same ship, or a different ship?

The most consequential thought experiment in American history, of course, was the one proposed in Philadelphia during the summer 1787: What is the best form of government? For five months, 55 of the Union's most accomplished statesmen, lawyers, writers, and citizens convened in one austere assembly room to craft the most celebrated document in human history. The creation of the document itself, however, was far from inevitable. On Monday, June 11—after just two weeks of debate—a spike in heated rhetoric threatened to derail the Convention entirely. William Patterson, a 41-year-old Irish immigrant serving as a delegate from New Jersey, expressed his staunch disagreement with the Virginia Plan by exclaiming that he would prefer to live under a monarch or despot than under James Madison's bicameral legislative proposal.

Sensing a cataclysm, a local 81-year-old printer named Benjamin Franklin decided to intervene. In fact,

---

* Kurzweil, pursuant to his Law of Accelerating Returns, has made 147 long-term technological predictions since the 1990s, fully 115 of which have turned out to be correct, while another 12 have turned out to be "essentially correct" (off by a year or two), giving his predictions a stunning 86 percent accuracy rate.

he had already prepared a speech for this very moment. When Patterson yielded the floor, Franklin slipped a piece of parchment into the hands of fellow Pennsylvania delegate James Wilson. Wilson then rose and, on Franklin's behalf, issued an elegant appeal to the delegates' better angels, calling on them to quiet their tempers and rededicate themselves to the ever-important task at hand:

> It has given me great pleasure to observe that till this point, . . . our debates were carried on with great coolness & temper. If any thing of a contrary kind, has on this occasion appeared, I hope it will not be repeated; for we are sent here to *consult*, not to *contend*, with each other; and declarations of a fixed opinion, and of determined resolution, never to change it, neither enlighten nor convince us. Positiveness and warmth on one side, naturally beget their like on the other; and tend to create and augment discord & division in a great concern, wherein harmony & Union are extremely necessary to give weight to our Councils, and render them effectual in promoting & securing the common good.

Though equally intense rhetoric would occasionally

find its way to the Convention floor in the coming months, Franklin's call for civility established a framework through which the delegates could engage in substantive yet respectful debate vis-à-vis the best means of achieving the common good. With civility as their guideposts, the delegates proceeded with a "yielding and accommodating spirit" to engage in the most profound display of rational discourse this continent has ever seen.[4] The end product was the Constitution, which, to this day, remains the custodian of American liberty.

In contemplating the Grand Convention and its role in history, one question that I often return to is this: Why were these 55 men so prepared for that moment? In other words, why is it that when the gods of history came calling, these men responded by climbing to the top of Mt. Reason and crafting a Constitution that, 230-plus years later, now seems angelic?

The answer, at first glance, seems quite simple. Reason requires training. And training requires education. And the Founders' education was grounded, above all, in a quest for the public good.

Despite our substantial progress, however, the end-goals of the Constitutional Convention—equality, prosperity, and justice for all—have yet to be realized. Indeed, at the present moment, it appears that the Founders' grand experiment has been infected with the life-threatening disease of constitutional decay. The question, then, is where did we go wrong?

* * *

With this book, I hope to offer a possible answer to this question. I do so in the spirit of Winston Churchill, whose 1938 work, *While England Slept*, ominously told of "how the English-speaking peoples through their unwisdom, carelessness, and good nature allowed the wicked to rearm." The book, which sat annotated on President Roosevelt's bedtime table, appeared well before Munich at a time when prevailing opinion held that Hitler had made his last demands. "The idea that dictators can be appeased by kind words and minor concessions is doomed to disappointment," he told the League of Nations Union on June 2, 1938. "Volcanic forces are moving in Europe, and sombre figures are now at the head of the most powerful races. The dictator countries are prepared night and day to advance their ambitions, if possible by peace, if necessary by war. I am under the impression that we and other countries stand in great danger."

I too believe that volcanic forces are moving, not only in Europe, but in the United States. The forces are of a different nature, though not entirely so. Like Europe in the 1930s, Americans today are blinded by propaganda and distracted by tactical diversion. Decades of truth decay have withered our country's moral and intellectual vitality. And calculated efforts to lull voters into a state of extreme apathy and ignorance have proved largely successful.

Of course, one can point to many causes for our current state of affairs, but I believe that the cornerstone to our predicament lies at the feet of Edward Bernays, the forefather of modern propaganda (later called "public relations") whose psychological tactics have been appropriated and expounded upon over the past century by American political and business forces alike. As an American psy-ops solider in World War I, Bernays learned that human beings could be manipulated into action by appealing to their irrational desires. After the War, he sold his toolkit of Freudian persuasion to everyone from Calvin Coolidge to the American Tobacco Company, who in turn convinced Americans with stunning success that individual choice and material accumulation were more important than communal equality and the pursuit of knowledge. The extent to which Bernays was able to transform America from a country of citizens into a country of consumers is, in my view, one of the most consequential peacetime developments of the twentieth century, and a story that I believe must be told if we are to avoid slipping further into unreality.

The Bernays phenomenon coincided with a calculated pursuit of vanity that, in my judgment, is best illustrated by the self-help phenomenon of Dale Carnegie, whose 1936 book *How to Win Friends and Influence People* is widely regarded as one of the most "influential" American works of the last century.

Though Carnegie's goals were certainly laudable, I believe that his vapid blueprint of salesmanship, which is premised on the notion that Americans can be convinced of the merits of an idea by influence rather than proof, is one of the major reasons for the dearth of critical thinking skills in American culture today.

The dawn of the Carnegie success model, combined with the proliferation of Bernays's propaganda techniques, have generated what I call a country of Bernagie (Bernays + Carnegie) thinkers—a mass assortment of advertisers and consumers who possess a devastating inability to identify deception and think critically about complex subjects. Our national vessel of unity, as a result, has been subsumed by an omniscient wave of materialism dedicated to the proposition that all men are created unequal. In this new kingdom of selfdom, progress is no longer synonymous with communal advancement; instead, progress is tantamount to material enrichment, a Pyrrhic ambition to be pursued at the expense of civic friendship and common duty. Democracy, as we know from the Founders, is incompatible with such hollow ambitions.

This confluence of circumstances, along with other factors of course, has produced a dangerous degree of bewilderment regarding our current state of affairs. As Sam Ervin once said, we have become "as foolish as the man who went bear hunting and stopped to chase rabbits." To solve our predicament and halt our descension into entropy, we must reorient ourselves and redefine our purpose. We must hunt bear and get bear. To do so, a few things are necessary.

First, we must relearn the political science underlying the construction of our government. We tend to think that a good government, once established, continues on forever unless it is destroyed by forces beyond our borders. We therefore pursue external defenses over internal safeguards without realizing that such an approach inverts the primary method of self-preservation endorsed by our Founders.

But despotism, like cancer, spreads from the inside out. Economic inequality yields intellectual apathy and political ferment fosters civic unrest. Chaos propagates, the future turns dark, and the present becomes dystopian. The Founding Fathers, more than anyone, feared this parlous progression. That democracy produced the modern world's most barbarous tyrants, *il duce* and the *führer,* would not have surprised them.

As we continue in our quest for the ideal, we would be wise to remember the lesson that Plato teaches us in the eighth book of the *Republic.* He tells us that all governments have a beginning, middle, and end. He warns us that decay comes inevitably to all civilizations in the form of self-love, which eventually overcomes society's soul and cripples its capacity for communal progress. Indeed, it is for this reason that all of world's greatest empires have fallen. Ask yourselves: *Est ubi Gloria nunc Babyloniae*? Where is the glory of Babylon now? Or ancient Rome, India, and Greece? And why should America escape a similar fate?

But Plato also teaches us that, if we're lucky, we may experience a democratic rebirth. Via reasoned judgment and civic friendship, we may ignite a great renewal; a modern version of democracy modeled after the Founders' utopic vision of a virtuous republic. To do so, we must come to understand that the Preamble to the Constitution is not an overture but an instruction. *We* the People *must* seek union, justice, tranquility, and liberty. These are the constituent parts of the common good; one cannot exist without the others, nor can they be obtained unless *we* do it together.

Our task will be difficult. But thankfully the Founders have provided to us the means and ends necessary to ignite a revolution. The means are found in the First Amendment—speech, assembly, press, and religion. They are our primary methods of persuasion and are available to each one of us as citizens. As Aristotle wrote more than two millennia ago, "The end and purpose of a polis is the good life, and the institutions of social life are means to that end."[5] Our tools of persuasion must be utilized to the greatest extent possible if we are to fulfill our perambulatory purpose. To maximize their persuasive power, we must implement a morally robust system of discourse grounded in a public philosophy of citizenship—from each according to his powers, to each according to his needs. The Constitution was devised for this very purpose. By engaging in the process of rational, public debate, the citizen discovers that more can be accomplished on a communal scale than one could ever hope to accomplish in isolation. The common good, as a result, merges with individual fulfillment, thus allowing the citizen and the community to march together in the pursuit of happiness.

If we are to be successful in the days ahead, if we are to rediscover our shared bonds of citizenship, then we must commit ourselves to the quest of the common good and the discipline of self-government. "Too much and too long," said Robert Kennedy, "we seem to have surrendered community excellence and community values in the mere accumulation of material things." At long last we must comprehend that material wealth "does not include the beauty of our poetry or the strength of our marriages; the intelligence of our public debate or the integrity of our public officials. It measures neither our wit nor our courage; neither our wisdom nor our learning; neither our compassion nor our devotion to our country; it measures everything, in short, except that which makes life worthwhile. And it tells us everything about America except why we are proud that we are Americans."[6]

But we must realize that history has forced upon us a fierce urgency of *now*. The future, my friends, is here. We have inherited the technological and scientific consequences propagated by two world wars and the advent of the corporate superpower. No other generation has been tasked with addressing radical climate change, genetic modification, artificial intelligence, surveillance capitalism, mass migration, global poverty, and the unremitting threat posed by nuclear and biological weapons. Sir Martin Rees, former President of the Royal Society and co-founder of the Centre for the Study of Existential Risk at the University of Cambridge, gives modern civilization a 50 percent chance of making it through the current century.[7] It is not hyperbole to say that the future rests on our shoulders. We therefore must accept the burden imposed upon us, because in the words of the poet Longfellow:

Humanity with all its fears,
With all its hopes of future years
Is hanging breathless on thy fate.

1
A REPUBLIC OF REASON

"The mind once enlightened cannot again become dark."

Thomas Paine

"The Constitution of the United States was written by fifty-five men—and one ghost," writes retired Army Lieutenant General Dave R. Palmer. The ghost was that of Oliver Cromwell.[8]

In 1641, an eight-year civil war broke out in England. Cromwell valiantly led the parliamentary forces against the monarchical King Charles I and, in 1653, became Lord Protector of England. His tenure began optimistically. The war-torn country longed for stability and its citizens hoped that Cromwell would provide to them the assurance of liberty. But as Theodore Roosevelt would write nearly 250 years later, Cromwell soon "acquired a dictatorial habit of mind" and became "cursed with the love of power." Combining "cruelty with ultimate inefficiency," Cromwell "devised a tyranny worse than any that ever existed under the English Kings."[9]

The Cromwellian era ended alongside the death of its leader in 1658. The monarchy reclaimed power shortly thereafter and succeeded for a brief period under King Charles II in restoring order. But tyranny soon returned. In 1688, another civil war broke out under the dictatorial rule of Charles's brother, James II. This time, Parliament was prepared. In what would become known as the "Glorious Revolution," Parliament ousted James II from the thrown and invited the Dutch *Statholder*, William of Orange, and his wife, Mary, to replace him. William subsequently agreed to relinquish many of the powers that had been bestowed upon previous kings, a decision that marked a historic transfer of power from the Crown to Parliament. A Bill of Rights was passed in 1689, igniting a spirit of optimism that would match that of the American Revolution roughly a century later.[10]

By the turn of the eighteenth century, however, corruption again started to seep from the halls of Westminster. In due time, staunch opponents of Parliament began to emerge on both sides of the Atlantic. The growing concern over the direction of English politics was fueled by publications like *Cato's Letters*—a series of 144 newspaper articles published between 1720-1723 by British writers John Trenchard and Thomas Gordon—which warned Americans and Brits alike that tyranny was afoot.*

Of the myriad forebodings published at the time, perhaps the best description of the impending political danger was that offered by British poet and playwright James Thomson. In a searing indictment of Prime Minister Robert ("Robin") Walpole, Thomson coined a new term to describe the dire state of affairs. A "Robinocracy," he wrote, had emerged in England. At the center of this new form of government was a

---

* The work's namesake is Cato the Younger (95-46 B.C.), the Roman champion of liberty who became the chief foe of Julius Caesar. After the British captured the American capital of Philadelphia in September 1777, George Washington—despite a congressional ban on theatrical productions—coordinated a showing of Joseph Addison's 1713 tragedy *Cato* at Valley Forge, which he hoped would improve Continental moral and inspire the soldiers' vigor for liberty. It worked, it seems.

"Robinarch" who had manufactured a façade of lawfulness while, behind the scenes, he surreptitiously sought to monopolize the entire system of government. Though nominally appointed by the prince, the Robinarch had in reality become a "sovereign" unto himself; "as despotic, arbitrary a sovereign as this part of the world affords." This corrupt Robinarch, Thomson seethed, had hijacked the government's commitment to liberty by encouraging "*luxury* and *extravagance*, the certain forerunners of *indigence*, *dependence*, and *servility*." And his profligate rule was reflected in his cadre of underlings, all of whom were:

> tied down with *honors*, *titles*, *preferments*, of which the *Robinarch* engrosse[d] the disposal to himself, and others with *bribes*. . . . Some [were] persuaded to prostitute themselves for the lean reward of *hopes* and *promises*; and others, more senseless than all of them, [had] sacrificed their principles and consciences to a set of *party names*, without any meaning, or the vanity of appearing in favor at *court*.[11]

This spirit of opposition was not lost on the

Founders.* Indeed, their pamphlets reveal that they sought to defeat the Robinarch via recourse to the teachings of those who had lived during or shortly after the fall of Rome—particularly Plutarch, Livy, Cicero, Sallust and Tacitus. A young John Dickinson, writing from London in 1754, wrote that England appeared to have modeled itself after Sallust's Rome: "Easy to be bought, if there was but a purchaser."[12] Like the Founders, these classical writers feared the trends of their own era and longed for an earlier age governed by liberty and justice.

More than any other writers, the ancients gave our forefathers the gift of inspiration and, equally important, provided them with insight as to what can happen when government runs awry. From Cicero, they learned that "the people's good is the highest law."[13] Plutarch instructed them to "rigorously to maintain liberty,"[14] the loss of which, as Livy forewarned, signified "the height of arbitrary government."[15] To obtain justice for all, they had to emulate Tactius, "an upright Patriot, zealous for publick Liberty and the welfare of his Country, and a delared

* In an ironic twist, Walpole would go on to play an important, albeit accidental, role in the crafting of the American Constitution. After being exiled from England, he found himself in the company of Montesquieu. During a conversation about government, Walpole suggested that Montesquieu inquire into a principle of government called "separation of powers." Montesquieu heeded Walpole's advice and incorporated the concept into his *Spirit of Laws*. James Madison, in turn, used Montesquieu's argument to convince his colleagues to adopt the tripartite system of government that we live with today.

enemy to Tyrants and to the instruments of Tyranny."[16]

Though they may not have realized it themselves, the Founders were no doubt children of antiquity. But while the classics provided the Founders with vision, it was the writings of Enlightenment rationalism that provided them with direction. As historian Bernard Bailyn observes, the sheer number of citations to leading Enlightenment thinkers in pamphlets from the era "is at times astonishing."[17] Devoid of the sort of emotional intensity that permeates today's public sphere, their exquisitely rational writings reveal a remarkable ability to communicate ideas. The French-American writer Hector St. John de Crèvecoeu summed it up best when he wrote that "the American . . . is a new man, who acts upon new principles, . . . entertain[s] new ideas and form[s] new opinions."[18] From their writings, it is clear that the Founders sought to *convince* their opponents, not conquer them.

That is not to say that the Founders were always in agreement, however. Quite the contrary. The Founders argued ad nauseam over the proper construction of Government: Federalists vs. Anti-Federalists, Madisonian liberals vs. Jeffersonian civic republicans, etc. But while they disagreed in their conclusions, they agreed in their fundamental premises—that answers were to be obtained through reason rather than revelation; that citizenship was a duty, not a title; and that government should always strive to improve public well-being.

In this sense, the Revolution was, at its core, a purely rational *weltanschauung*. The era's thinkers—most of whom were "eclectics, skeptics, anticlericals, scientists, religious exiles, and journalists"—combined logic with empirical observation to deduce the best means of expanding knowledge and securing the common good. They adhered to the principle that you have to *prove* what you say; spouting blatant untruths, appealing to the divine, or launching ad hominem attacks was simply out of bounds.[19]

Of the numerous Enlightenment writers whose work influenced the Founders, three in particular loom large in the drafting of the Constitution: Thomas Hobbes, John Locke, and Charles-Louis de Secondat, Baron de La Brède et de Montesquieu. Each shared in common a rational approach to politics. They flatly rejected mysticism and disavowed the age-old view that the state is divinely ordained. And while each endorsed their own conclusions of human nature, they nevertheless agreed that man is a product of his environment and may, with proper instruction, be taught the ability to reason.

A number of the Founders endorsed Hobbesian views of society, the most conspicuous of which was Alexander Hamilton. Human beings, according to Hobbes, are often blinded by passion. They seek near-term advantages at the expense of their own long-term interests. They are vulnerable to impulse and prone to violence. Without government, Hobbes wrote, life is "solitary, poor, nasty, brutish, and short."[20]

Thankfully, the Founders did not subscribe to Hobbes's belief that the Leviathan—Hobbes's term for an all-powerful authoritarian state—is the only type of government capable of controlling human vanities. But they were nevertheless influenced by Hobbes's skepticism of human nature, especially with regard to the exercise of political power. In fact, just a week after Benjamin Franklin issued his memorable call for civility, Hamilton stood before the Convention and made an impassioned plea for an aristocratic government. Echoing Hobbes, he argued to his fellow delegates that man was too corrupt for self-rule. "Most individuals" and "all public bodies," he declared, are governed by "the passions . . . of avarice, ambition, [and] interest."[21] With appropriate caveats, political prudence demanded that "every man ought to be supposed a *knave*; and to have no other end, in all his actions, but *private interest*. By this interest we must govern him, . . . notwithstanding his insatiable avarice and ambition."[22]

Even James Madison, whose political philosophy was more in line with Jefferson's liberalism than Hobbes's pessimism, expressed concerns about human character: "In all very numerous assemblies, of whatever character composed, passion never fails to wrest the sceptre from reason. Had every Athenian citizen been a Socrates, every Athenian assembly still would have been a mob."[23] Madison's Hobbesian concerns about human nature undergirded his support for the system of "checks and balances," which he saw as a necessary safeguard against man's inherent lack of goodness. In a memorable passage, Madison defended this proposition in the *Federalist* (No. 51):

> It may be a reflection on human nature, that such devices should be necessary to control the abuses of government. But what is government itself, but the greatest of all reflections on human nature? If men were angels, no government would be necessary. If angels were to govern men, neither external nor internal controls on government would be necessary. In framing a government which is to be administered by men over men, the great difficulty lies in this: you must first enable the government to control the governed; and in the next place oblige it to control itself.

But despite Hobbes's considerable sway, his cynical views on human nature did not prevail. Instead it was John Locke's political theory of natural rights and his spirited defense of human goodness that had the greatest influence on the Founders. In fact, Locke's *Essay Concerning Human Understanding* was popular not just among the Founders, but all Americans. 45 percent of personal libraries, it is believed, housed Locke's *Essay* on their bookshelves.[24] Many Americans were thus intimately familiar with Locke's contention that ideas are not the innate byproduct of human nature but instead a distinct outgrowth of experience. "Let us suppose," Locke posited, that the mind is "void of all characters, without any ideas; How comes it to be furnished?" For Locke, the answer was, "in one word, from experience. In that all our knowledge is founded; and from that it ultimately derives itself."[25]

Consider for a brief moment how profound this inquiry is. In the final analysis, the Founders subscribed not to the Hobbesian or even Christian view that human beings are fundamentally evil but rather to the Lockean view that human beings are the products of their environments. The logical extension of the Founders' beliefs is that a good environment can create virtuous citizens. In Lockean terms, citizens' minds are blank slates, *tabula rasae,* which can be taught, through proper education, the means of effective citizenship. As we continue exploring the Founders' vision for America, keep in mind that they deemed human beings capable of reasoned judgment and drafted the Constitution accordingly.

It was through this lens of philosophical idealism that the Founders turned to the most significant of Locke's teachings: his theory of natural rights. According to Locke, human beings possess in their pre-social state certain natural rights. Of those, the most important are their rights to life, liberty, and property.[26] When a person enters into a social state—that is, when one consents to be governed by a sovereign—he or she relinquishes certain natural privileges, including, for instance, the "power to punish offenses against the law of nature."[27] But in return, the state promises to protect that person's rights to life, liberty, and property. If the state violates that promise, then the citizen—having entered into a contract with the state—has the right to resist and, where necessary, void the agreement. In other words, the citizen may exercise his or her right to revolution.

The quintessential expression of Locke's ideas came, of course, from Thomas Jefferson, who wrote in the Declaration of Independence: "We hold these truths to be self-evident: that all men are created equal; that they are endowed by their Creator with certain inalienable rights; that among these are life, liberty, and pursuit of happiness." Though this sentence is certainly a nod to Locke, it is equally a nod to reason. To be sure, Jefferson's original draft began by stating: "We hold these truths to be *sacred and undeniable. . . .*" Benjamin Franklin, by substituting "self-evident" for "sacred and undeniable," transformed the Declaration from a received truth into a rational truth; a self-evident verity derived from solely from reason.[28]

Montesquieu was the third great influencer of the Revolution. His *Spirit of Laws* offered the Founders a persuasive critique of government; one rooted in the teachings of antiquity and the lessons of history. From those sources, Montesquieu discovered that, in the course of human affairs, three types of government tend to emerge: the despotic, ruled by "fear;" the monarchical, governed by "honor;" and the republic, characterized by "virtue."

A virtuous republic, Montesquieu explained, hinges on the education of its citizenry. Virtue in this context means political virtue in the citizen; not facile patriotism but a genuine, learned concern for all parts of the common good. Education has a similar meaning. It entails, through formal schooling, the acquisition of moral and intellectual virtues, which in turn must be cultivated and applied in civic life.[29]

But this form of education is not natural. Nor is it easy to obtain. It requires "a constant preference of public to private interest;" it "limits ambition to the sole desire, to the sole happiness, of doing greater services to our country than the rest of our fellow citizens;" and it "is a self-renunciation, which is ever arduous and painful." Democracy, in other words, is an onerous task. To foster a genuine concern for the common good, "the whole power of democracy is required." Otherwise, the citizenry will become corrupted. Private interests will replace the public good, and power will be sought for its own sake. Eventually the government will cease to function, and virtue will vanish from whence it came.[30]

To safeguard liberty and ensure the preservation of political virtue, Montesquieu advocated for the implementation of three distinct branches of government: the executive, the legislative, and the judicial. He believed that if the same person or political body were left to oversee, enact, and enforce the laws of the land, "there would be an end of everything." James Madison reiterated the necessity for a division of powers in the *Federalist* (No. 47) when he declared that "the accumulation of all powers, legislative, executive, and judiciary, in the same hands, whether of one, a few, or many, and whether hereditary, selfappointed, or elective, may justly be pronounced the very definition of tyranny." By adhering to a system of checks and balances, Montesquieu believed that each branch could act as a check on the others, thereby ensuring the quest for the common good.

* * *

With this background in mind, it can be seen that the Constitution, rather than endorsing one particular philosophy over another, is a zetetic construction. It is an embodiment of the human mind itself. The fact that it even exists in the first place is, as Madison noted, a reflection of man's Hobbesian fallibility; "if men were angels, no government would be necessary." But it is also a document of audacious hope. By its very structure, it gives mankind an opportunity to pursue the ideal state. Armed with their natural rights of life, liberty, and the pursuit of happiness, the Constitution provides for its citizens a road toward fulfillment. Through proper education and reasoned judgment, Americans may come to develop a love for the common good. And if their elected representatives lead them astray, the citizens may exercise their right to revolution.

The Constitution, in other words, is emblematic of the Founders' breathtaking vision for America. It gives the body politic a resonance unmatched in human history; one grounded in reason, civic duty, and sacrifice. The delegates who met in Philadelphia during the summer of 1787 personified this approach to governance. Despite great differences in opinion, they nevertheless held in common certain sentiments regarding the public philosophy of citizenship—as Thomas Paine put it, they had "common sense." They understood that no particular individual was more important than the collective body, and in this spirit of civility, they worked together toward the creation of a more perfect union.

At the core of the Founders' political genius was their ability to persuade. The word itself is the favorite verb of Thucydides in the *Peloponnesian War* and of Plato in the *Republic*. As the Greeks understood it, persuasion (as a verb) meant faith; "faith in right opinion, faith in physical science, faith in persons and institutions, and the good faith of the man of character, the faith that can submit itself to Socratic criticism in order to arrive at its own understanding."[31] Persuasion, under this definition, is the process by which law is ordained; an exploration of reasons that rests as much on the ability to persuade as it does on the willingness to be persuaded. The main ingredients of persuasion are found, naturally, in the First Amendment—speech, press, assembly, and religion. The First Amendment is the guardian of persuasion; without it, reason is evanescent.

By definition, persuasion enlists human beings for the common pursuit of an end.[32] The Constitutional Convention, in this sense, was a pure exercise in the art of persuasion. In fact, the same can be said for the post-Convention ratification process as well. For more than a year, a war of persuasion played out both on paper and in public as the Federalists and Anti-Federalists endeavored to convince colonial Americans on the merits of ratification. Though the Federalists would carry the day, the Anti-Federalist cause was not lost. To alleviate Anti-Federalist concerns of excessive federal power, the Federalists, led by Madison, agreed to add to the Constitution a list of ten amendments designed to secure the basic rights and privileges of American citizens. Had it not been for the Anti-Federalists' persuasive efforts, the Constitution would have been signed into law without a Bill of Rights.[33*]

* In fact, Madison was so persuaded by the Anti-Federalists' call for a Bill of Rights that he proposed an additional amendment of his own, one that sought to protect certain individual rights from state infringement: "No State shall infringe the equal rights of conscience, nor the freedom of

But was it wrong for the Founders to assume that future generations would follow in their footsteps? Alexander Hamilton, in the very first of the *Federalist* papers, pondered this very question when he asked "whether societies of men are really capable or not of establishing good government from reflection and choice, or whether they are forever destined to depend for their political constitutions on accident and force."

Herein lies our mission: Are we capable of establishing good government from reflection and choice? The world as an idea of reason is not merely a fool's fable; it is a practical imperative. History forced upon the Founders the ultimate task of choosing from all possible worlds the one realm that would allow mankind to flourish, and to make it so. The Founders understood that failure in this regard would be to vindicate Hobbes and confound god. Yet they did not cower at their awesome responsibility. Through reasoned debate and civil collaboration, the Founders decided that *our* government—a just government derived from the rational consent of the governed—best conformed to man's natural state.

Whether we possess the capacity to assume this heavy duty, however, remains unanswered. The

---

speech, or of the press, nor of the right of trial by jury in criminal cases." Madison's proposal passed in the House, but was voted down in the Senate, which favored a Bill of Rights that restrained the federal government only. The Constitutional Bill of Rights, as a result, would not apply to the states until the passing of the Fourteenth Amendment seventy-nine years later.

American experiment, despite our substantial progress, has flirted with failure on several occasions. The ideal not only remains unattained, it seems at the present moment to be slipping from our grasp. If we do not act, we shall never have the satisfaction of realizing our potential as a nation. We therefore must wake reason from her slumber, rededicate ourselves to the process of reasoned debate, and commit ourselves anew to the fulfillment of the common good. And this endeavor must begin, as the Founders instructed, in the classroom.

2
THE EDUCATIONAL DILEMMA

"Reason only knows what it has succeeded in learning."

Fyodor Dostoevsky

As George Washington assumed the presidency in 1789, optimism reigned supreme. Despite the Founders' awesome responsibility, they viewed with excitement the challenge of nurturing into existence a country replete with virtuous citizens. As historian Richard Hofstadter wrote, they viewed "the United States [as] the only country in the world that began with perfection and aspired to progress."[34] Indeed they had learned from Locke that the human mind, though ignorant in its natural state, was capable of being molded into a beacon of rectitude. "Human nature is the same in all ages and countries," said Dr. Benjamin Rush, "and all the differences we perceive in its characters in respect to virtue and vice, knowledge and ignorance, may be accounted for from climate, country, degrees of civilization, forms of government, or accidental causes."[35] By combining the exercise of reason with an unwavering commitment to "habitual virtue," the revolutionaries saw the potential of the young republic as truly limitless.[36] For them, the only challenge was: Where do we start?

The Founders had learned from their Enlightenment forbearers that virtue was the lynchpin of an effective republic. But unlike their forbearers, who tended to see government as the source of civic consciousness, the Founders were defenders of a more modern source of virtue: society. With the ghosts of Oliver Cromwell and the Robinarch still fresh in their minds, the young nation's more liberal-minded statesmen remained wary of whether government could adequately care for the well-being of its citizens. James Wilson, for example, took the Hobbesian view that government was "highly necessary," but only because of man's "fallen state." Wilson believed that society, and "particularly domestick society," offered a "better" arena for engaging in "the pleasures and virtues" of citizenship.[37] In this new community of benevolence, Wilson believed that citizens would "begin to know one another" and, in that process, acquire true "knowledge [that] begets a love for each other, and a desire to procure happiness for themselves, and the great family of mankind."[38]

Having immersed themselves in the study of philosophy, the Founders naturally recognized that the midwife to virtue was education. As America's first polymath class, the Founders were zealous advocates of learning. They believed, as the saying goes, that the man who doesn't read has no advantage over the man who can't. Of the fifty-five delegates who attended the Constitutional Convention, more than half had been educated at colleges in America or Europe, primarily in England. Others, like Benjamin Franklin and George Washington, had earned their Ph.Ds in the field of self-education. Each man dedicated himself to the process of lifelong learning and thereby developed habits of the mind that had previously belonged only to elite minorities.[39] They were, in other words, the first generation of gentlemen, a term that, unlike today, signaled decency, not pomposity. In the words of John

Adams, "gentlemen" did not mean "the rich or the poor, the high-born or the low-born, the industrious or the idle; but all those who have received a liberal education, an ordinary degree of erudition in liberal arts and sciences, whether by birth they be descended from magistrates and officers of government, or from husbandmen, merchants, mechanics, or laborers; or whether they be rich or poor."[40]

Fittingly, Franklin and Washington—both of whom lacked the benefit of formal schooling—were the era's champions of education. In 1749, nearly thirty years before he would come to preside over the Constitutional Convention, Benjamin Franklin wrote an influential pamphlet in which he argued for the adoption of a liberal curriculum designed to cultivate "a useful Culture of young Minds." At the core of this regimen was an emphasis on reason. In order to nurture this ability, Franklin proposed that students "debate in Conversation and in Writing" the various "[q]uestions of Right and Wrong, Justice and Injustice," that "naturally arise" in the course of human affairs. He believed that through this process, students "will begin to feel the Want, and be sensible of the *Use of Logic,* or the Art of Reasoning to *discover* Truth, and of Arguing to *defend* it, and *convince* Adversaries." Equally important, they will learn to avoid "consult[ing] *Custom* more than *Reason,*" and thus will elude "the Dangers and Inconveniencies of blindly following the Footsteps of those who have gone before [them]. . . ."[41]

George Washington, like Franklin, recognized that the success of America's young democracy depended in large part on citizens' pursuit of a liberal education. A modern day Cincinnatus, Washington told his congressional colleagues during his first annual address "that there is nothing which can better deserve your patronage than the promotion of science and literature. Knowledge is in every country the surest basis of public happiness." In a country like America where "the measures of government receive their impressions so immediately from the sense of the community," it was critical, Washington emphasized, that Americans be taught the tools of effective citizenship, including the capacity:

> to know and to value their own rights; to discern and provide against invasions of them; to distinguish between oppression and the necessary exercise of lawful authority; between burthens proceeding from a disregard to their convenience and those resulting from the inevitable exigencies of society; to discriminate the spirit of liberty from that of licentiousness—cherishing the first, avoiding the last—and uniting a speedy but temperate vigilance against encroachments, with an inviolable respect to the laws.[42]

Washington, like the Romans, understood "liberal" in its original Latin sense, "of or pertaining to free men." He hoped that by making a liberal education available to the masses, he could secure "a free constitution" and thereby answer Aristotle's criticism of democracy—that an uneducated and uniformed citizenry would lead to its ruin.

Washington thus became the country's leading advocate for a nationwide system of public education. His plan for obtaining "right education" was twofold. The first phase involved what we think of today as elementary and secondary education. It was intended to "provide children with the capacity to reason for themselves," a skill that Washington deemed necessary for obtaining "broad knowledge . . . through liberal studies." The second phase concerned higher learning. Via the allocation of federal land grants, Washington hoped to create public universities where students could simultaneously pursue specialized training in a particular area of study as well as receive instruction in "the science of government."

For Washington, the social component attendant to higher learning was as important as the education itself. As he wrote to Alexander Hamilton, bringing young leaders together in a community of learning would allow them to "discover that there was not . . . cause for those jealousies and prejudices which one part of the Union had imbibed against another part."[43] By building schools where politeness and benevolence were prioritized as much as scholarship, Washington hoped that students would emerge not only more educated, but more civil toward one another as well. His vision, in other words, was one of human decency.[44]

Washington's educational philosophy fit the *zeitgeist* of the era. "The business of education," wrote Benjamin Rush in 1798, "has acquired a new complexion by the independence of our country. The form of government we have assumed has created a new class of duties to every American." Citing "the principle of patriotism," Rush deemed it necessary to establish "nurseries of wise and good men, to adapt our modes of teaching to the peculiar form of our government."[45]

Thomas Jefferson's views echoed those of Washington and Rush. As a student at the College of William and Mary, he "heard more good sense, more rational and philosophical conversations than all my life besides."[46] After he graduated, however, he became disenchanted with the direction of the school's leadership. So in 1776, he devised a plan transform the character of the college entirely. His proposed curriculum included "Indian culture and language, modern languages, history, law, botany, chemistry, astronomy, mathematics, moral philosophy, natural philosophy, natural history, medicine and ancient languages." The school was to be governed by a board of directors, who in turn would be overseen by the Virginia state legislature. Though Jefferson initially struggled to convince the General Assembly to adopt his plan, he had more success after ascending to the Governorship in 1779. At that time, Jefferson replaced the College's board of directors and brought in new faculty members to teach several of the subjects that he had proposed in his original curriculum.* 40 years later, this liberal curriculum would serve as the model for the new curriculum implemented at the University of Virginia.[47]

* * *

Historian Gordon Wood writes that for Washington, Rush, and Jefferson—as well as many of their contemporaries—"adopting republicanism was not simply a matter of bringing American culture more into line with the society. It also meant an opportunity to abolish what remained of monarchy and to create once and for all new, enlightened republican relationships among people."[48] By devising a liberal curriculum that prioritized both reason and practical knowledge, the Founders had faith that the next generation would be prepared to engage collectively in business, politics, and citizenship without pitting one interest against the other. Indeed, they had reason to be hopeful. Colonial

* That same year, Jefferson proposed another bill to the Virginia legislature, A Bill for the More General Diffusion of Knowledge, which called for the implementation of a three-tiered educational system intended to provide a minimum level of education to the masses. The bill failed to garner the requisite votes, however, and was never passed.

America may very well have been the most literate society in world history at that point. This was particularly true in New England, where some estimates suggest that 70 to 100 percent of citizens were literate at the time of the American Revolution.[49]

A major part of the Founders' republican transition involved transforming "subjects" into "citizens." The part and parcel of this realignment was an emphasis on civic virtue. Men of special talent were asked to forgo, at least for a time, their pursuit of more lucrative endeavors in exchange for serving the public. The byproduct of this sacrifice, it was hoped, would be the creation of a new American cosmopolitan. In the words of Thomas Paine, this moral commitment to cosmopolitanism required one to "view things as they are, without regard to place or person." In this new world of charity, the only "religion" was "to do good."[50]

Washington, more than anyone, understood that the inculcation of civic virtue was a prerequisite to the development of a citizenry capable of self-government. In this sense, his desire to secure nationwide access to education was not only a political battle, but a battle over the vision of American society itself. It combined the liberal principles of knowledge, reason, and individual rights with a republican emphasis on the duties of citizenship. Above all, Washington viewed "institutions for the general diffusion of knowledge" as "an object of primary importance." In his farewell address, Washington offered a public valediction to the American people in which he reminded them that "virtue or morality is a necessary spring of popular government. . . . In proportion as the structure of a government gives force to public opinion, it is essential that public opinion should be enlightened."[51]

Washington, however, never got his educational wish. Though Jefferson and Madison each attempted to push public education bills through Congress, the idea of a centralized system of education—and particularly one funded by federal dollars—was anathema to most of their colleagues.[52] The naiveté that allowed the Federalists to pursue, with deep sincerity, the construction of a virtuous, educated republic soon proved to be one of their greatest shortcomings. The Anti-Federalists, led by the likes of Melancton Smith of New York and William Petrikin of Pennsylvania, offered a different conception of America that proved far more appealing to the young nation.

For this oft-forgotten group of Founding Fathers, the Washingtonian position outlined above—i.e., that government could be comprised of virtuous, disinterested statesmen taught to pursue the common good—was patently absurd. Society, they believed, was not a homogenous body dedicated to a common purpose but rather a heterogeneous medley of "different classes or orders of people, Merchants, Farmers, Planters, Mechanics, and Gentry or wealthy Men."[53] Given this widespread diversity, the Anti-

Federalists believed it impossible for America to be represented by a single Enlightened class. To more faithfully represent the citizenry, they called for a true democracy; the "most explicit form of representation possible."[54] To impose any other form of government, wrote the *Federal Farmer*, would be to mislead the American people: "It is deceiving the people to tell them they are electors, and can choose their legislators, if they cannot in the nature of things, choose men among themselves, and genuinely like themselves."[55]

The knock-on effects of the Anti-Federalists' position were both far-reaching and immediate. The Federalists soon realized that they had neither the financial means nor the manpower to marshal in their goal of a virtuous republic.[56] Jefferson, realizing this misalignment between reality and expectation, united with the Anti-Federalists in the early 1790s to create the Democratic-Republican Party—the party of the "common man."[57] By the time Washington stepped down in 1797, government had become a bazaar of competing interests. National concerns were upstaged by a litany of local, partisan affairs that were rarely compatible with one another. Without a virtuous class in power to ensure that politicians pursued the common good, private interests became the chief concern for the nation's representatives.

But Washington's educational cause was not lost. During the late eighteenth and early nineteenth centuries, a number of state legislatures responded to calls for increased access to higher education by chartering their own colleges and universities. Massachusetts, New Hampshire, Connecticut, South Carolina, North Carolina, Kentucky, Virginia, New Jersey, Maryland, Pennsylvania, Georgia, and New York all chartered state institutions of higher learning. The schools' curricula, by and large, was demonstrably liberal—they prioritized religious tolerance, secular reasoning, and the teaching of republican virtues.[58] As Jefferson eventually realized in 1818, "there was more work to be done in . . . teaching citizens the connection between their own well-being and the political health of the county, than he had hitherto realized."[59] In due time, schools across the country began opening their doors to women and African Americans as well. Between 1837 and the outbreak of the Civil War in 1861, the United States—led by Oberlin College, a private liberal arts school in Ohio—went from having zero coeducational institutions to more than 20. The Institute for Colored Youth, the first higher education institution for African Americans, was founded in Cheyney, Pennsylvania, in 1837. Two more black institutions—Lincoln University in 1854 and Wilberforce University in 1856—followed thereafter.[60]

Alongside increased access to liberal education came remarkable advancements in civic society that mirrored those of ancient Greece. In their heyday, Athenians enjoyed a deep, intimate relationship with their city; indeed, from Aristotle we learn that the

Athenians had a word for those who refused to participate in public affairs: *idiotes*. In the city of Athens, civic participation was required and neither apathy nor aloofness was condoned. "The man who took no interest in the affairs of state was not a man who minded his own business," wrote Thucydides, "but a man who had no business being in Athens at all."[61]

The Athenians would have been proud of the American lyceum movement. In 1826, the small town of Millbury, Massachusetts, began holding evening educational lectures that were open to members of the local community, free of charge. The movement took on a life of its own, and within five years, the United States—with a population of only 13 million—was home to roughly 1,000 town lyceums.[62] From Detroit to Florida, notable public figures including Ralph Waldo Emerson, Susan B. Anthony, Emma Willard, Mark Twain, Oliver Wendell Holmes, Henry David Thoreau, Abraham Lincoln, Frederick Douglass, Elizabeth Cady Stanton, and William Lloyd Garrison traveled the lyceum circuit giving speeches and lectures to local men, women, and children of all colors and creeds.[63] With lecturers donating their time for free, organizers were able to keep costs at a minimum, thus providing low-income citizens with affordable access to meaningful education.[64]

The Father of the American lyceum movement was a Yale-educated scientist named Josiah Holbrook. Under his leadership, the American lyceum cemented itself as a pillar of civic engagement. "Americans of all ages, all conditions, and all minds," wrote Alexis de Tocqueville, "are constantly joining together in groups. . . . [They] have lately perfected the art of pursuing their common desires in common and [have] applied this new science to the largest number of objects."[65] The U.S. Office of Education, looking back on the lyceum movement at the turn of the nineteenth century, described Holbrook's enterprise as "a republican or patriotic institution" dedicated to "the universal diffusion of knowledge, which has ever been considered the strongest and surest, if not the only, foundation of republican government." Through "neighborly good will" and "universal benevolence," the lyceum fostered a spirit of civility where "men and women felt bound to add to the common stock of human happiness. . . ."[66]

From our twenty-first century perspective, it is difficult to comprehend the impact, in early nineteenth century terms, that the public forum had on American society. We receive our information today via pre-packaged, audiovisual sound bites and 280-character tweets, neither of which requires one to expend any brainpower in order to gauge the legitimacy of the claim presented. Our public dialogue, in other words, is both isolated and one-sided—people shout at us and we shout back, but no one actually listens.

Holbrook's lyceum, by contrast, was both interactive and pedagogical. The lecturers presented detailed evidence to the audience in support of a particular claim, and the audience, in turn, was then afforded an opportunity to ask questions and challenge assertions. This interactive form of engagement was particularly powerful in terms of advancing the overlapping causes of abolition and women's suffrage. Guardians of the status quo were forced to confront, often for the first time, the baseness of their moral defects. America's first female advocates of abolition and women's rights, Sarah and Angelina Grimké, drew massive audiences as they traveled across the country speaking on the dual evils of slavery and gender oppression. Reflecting on her December 4, 1837, address before a crowd of 1,500 people at the Boston Lyceum, Angelia Grimké noted: "The discussion has raised my hopes of the woman question. It was conducted with respect, delicacy, and dignity, and many minds no doubt were roused to reflection. . . ." A few months later, two Boston women, inspired by the Grimké sisters' spellbinding oration, created the first Bostonian newspaper dedicated to the advancement of women's rights.[67]

This era of moral and intellectual progress dovetailed with a period of American government that, despite early growing pains, nevertheless made significant strides toward the creation of a more perfect Union. With persons like Jefferson in the presidency, Daniel Webster and Henry Clay in the legislature, and John Marshall in the judiciary, our tripartite system of government functioned, by and large, as intended. Each branch debated and expounded upon the implied powers of the Constitution, and through the art of persuasion, they propelled America onto the world stage as a leader in both political science and jurisprudence.

The Senate in particular was home to some of "the most celebrated Americans" of the age. In response to what they correctly perceived to be flagrant abuses of executive power on the part of Andrew Jackson, Senators Webster and Clay voiced their oppositions to the president and his supporters by turning the Senate into "the central arena" for political debate.[68] Throughout the 1830s, men and women flocked to the Capitol to hear the "Great Triumvirate" of Webster, Clay, and Senator John C. Calhoun speak on the most pressing issues of the era. As historian Merrill D. Peterson writes: "All across the country their speeches were read as if the fate of the nation hung on them; and whether in Washington, at home, or on the road they could never escape the noisy pomp of fame."[69] The Senators' oratorical exquisiteness was not lost on Alexis de Tocqueville, who noted during his celebrated visit to the U.S. Capitol in 1832 that the Senate was comprised of "eloquent advocates, distinguished generals, wise magistrates and statesmen of note, whose language would at times do honor to the most remarkable parliamentary debates in Europe."[70]

Not surprisingly, the public's oratory adoration

soon trickled down into the classrooms. The Great Triumvirate's reign in the Senate coincided with a common school movement that, by 1840, had reached its zenith. This overlapping emphasis on education and oration led to one textbook—*McGuffey's Readers*—dominating the schoolbook market for much of the nineteenth century. Indeed, so influential were *McGuffey's Readers* that, outside of the King James Bible, they "were the most widely read book in 19th-century America."[71]

In stark contrast to today's educational tutorials, *McGuffey's Readers* invoked an Aristotelian model of rhetoric that aimed to teach girls and boys how "to read *aloud* deliberately and correctly" (emphasis mine). In order to practice their oration, students often memorized famous speeches given by America's best patriot-orators—Daniel Webster's "Against Hayne," Patrick Henry's "Give me liberty or give me death," and James Otis's "Against the writs of assistance," to name a few.[72] Through this process, students learned to interpret, rather than merely repeat, the words that they read. In doing so, they came to comprehend that language "should be looked at as a medium, not as an end."[73]

Students continued to refine their oratory skills as they made their way through secondary school and into college, where the study of rhetoric merged with lessons in language and literature. Though the curricula was diverse across the various institutions, most schools paired classical works like Cicero's *De Oratore* and Horace's *Ars Poetica* alongside more contemporary works like John Quincy Adams's *Lectures on Rhetoric and Oratory*. The latter in particular prioritized what Adams described as "the art of persuasion." According to Adams, persuasion is an art because "persuasion is not necessarily [the orator's] aim." To the contrary, "[t]he aim of the speaker must be to produce conviction, rather than persuasion; to operate by proof, rather than by influence."[74] Perhaps recalling Plato's criticism of the Sophists,* Adams emphasized that, above all, "the drift of the argument is to justice; not to utility." The brilliant Edward Tyrrel Channing—who succeeded Adams as the Boylston Professor of Rhetoric and Oratory at Harvard—likewise told his students that an orator should not be a "leader of the multitude" but instead should consider himself "one of the multitude, deliberating with them upon common interests."[75]

One of the hidden marvels of the oratory era was that, in addition to its emphasis on pursuing the common good, it produced statesmen with a wonderful capacity for savvy repartee. Susan Jacoby, in her book *The American Unreason,* notes that the oratory generation's capacity for sophisticated wit would put our generation to shame. Whereas politicians today tend to imitate the verbal inventiveness of Dick

* "When a person supposes that he knows, and does not know; this appears to be the great source of all the errors of the intellect" (Plato, *Sophist*, 229c).

Cheney—who in 2004, while presiding as president of the Senate, told Senator Patrick Leahy, "Go fuck yourself"—the politicians of the nineteenth century delivered far more nuanced and devastating jabs against their opponents. In the 1890s, for example, Speaker of the House Thomas Reed delivered a knock-out blow to a congressional colleague by observing that "with a few more brains he could be a halfwit." Of another politician, Reed quipped, "He never opens his mouth without subtracting from the sum of human intelligence."[76] And when asked if the Republican Party might nominate him for the presidency, Reed replied, "They could do worse, and they probably will."[77] Naturally, Reed was a graduate of Bowdoin College, a liberal arts institution in Maine. It was there he learned, in his own words, that "eloquence is inspiration. It is the highest flight of genius and commands the loftiest ambitions of the human mind. Deep thought, quick wit, and a steady earnestness of purpose can accomplish it."[78]

* * *

It was during this period of magnificent oration that Horace Mann, America's "educator of century," emerged on the scene. Born in Massachusetts to a family of farmers in May 1796, Mann fashioned himself in the mold of a young Benjamin Franklin, spending his days in a relentless quest for self-improvement at the fittingly named Franklin Public Library. With his innate curiosity and learned work ethic, Mann eventually earned an acceptance to Brown University in 1816, where he graduated as valedictorian. The title of his valedictory, "The Progressive Character of the Human Race," would soon become his life's motto.

After spending a few years practicing law in Boston, Mann entered the Massachusetts legislature in 1827, where he spent the better part of the next eight years—first as a state representative and then as president of the senate. He would later go on to represent Massachusetts as an anti-slavery Whig in the House of Representatives from 1848 to 1853, taking the seat vacated by the death of John Quincy Adams.*

As someone who described himself as having a "love of knowledge that nothing could repress," it was only natural that Mann, in 1837, became Massachusetts' first Secretary of Education, a position that he accepted with grace and humility: "A new fountain may now be opened. Let me strive to direct its current in such a manner, that if, when I have departed from life, I may still be permitted to witness its course, I may behold it broadening and deepening in an everlasting progression of virtue and happiness. Henceforth, so long as I hold this office, I devote myself to the

* In his first speech to Congress in 1848, Mann delivered prescient remarks on the impending battle over slavery: "I think the country is to experience serious times. Interference with slavery will excite civil commotion in the South. But it is best to interfere. Now is the time to see whether the Union is a rope of sand or a band of steel."

supremest welfare of mankind upon earth."

A staunch advocate for equal access to opportunity, Mann possessed a firm conviction that America's future depended "upon the best common school education for those who need it most." Indeed, his belief in educational reform was so strong that he gave up his lucrative law practice to assume the role of Secretary. As he transitioned from the practice of law into the field of education, his watchword became, "Let the next generation be my client."[79]

Mann's first common school opened in Lexington on July 3, 1839. From that point forward, Mann sought to teach children of all religious, class, and ethnic backgrounds (particularly the foreign-born) how to engage in the intelligent and responsible exercise of citizenship.[80] He believed—like Washington and Jefferson before him—that the only way to inculcate the requisite traits of virtue and benevolence was to develop students' "faculty of reason, whose especial office and function [is] to discover the connection between causes and effects; and thereby to enable us to regulate the causes of to-day, as to predestinate the effects of to-morrow."[81] Like all good educators, Mann knew that if America's youth lacked the capacity to reason their way through complex dilemmas in order to ascertain the common good, the American experiment itself would be but a star-crossed voyage of injustice and inequality:

> In a republican government the ballot-box is the urn of fate; yet no god shakes the bowl or presides over the lot. If the ballot-box is open to wisdom and patriotism and humanity, it is equally open to ignorance and treachery, to pride and envy, to contempt for the poor, or hostility toward the rich. . . . [But] if the votes, which fall so copiously into the ballot-box, on our days of election, emanate from wise counsels and a loyalty to truth, they will descend, like benedictions from heaven, to bless the land and fill it with song and gladness, such as has never been known upon earth since the days of paradise.[82]

Over time, Mann developed a blueprint of equality that contained two overlapping emphases. The first was educational. Students were schooled in the liberal subjects of philosophy, economics, history, religion, mathematics, science, law, and literature. The second emphasis was ethical. In his now famous Twelfth Annual Report of 1848, Mann advised educators to teach the "principles of piety, justice, and sacred regard to truth, love to their country, humanity and universal benevolence, sobriety, industry, frugality, chastity, moderation, and temperance, and those other virtues which are the ornament of human society, and the basis upon which a republican constitution is founded."[83] By combining individual intellect with universal comity, Mann hoped to foster a new "public philosophy"—one in which Americans moved in lockstep with one another toward the attainment of the common good.[84] Mann's lifelong quest in this regard was best captured in the parting words he gave to students at Antioch College shortly before his death in 1859: "Be ashamed to die until you have won some victory for humanity."[85]

Mann's tax-supported movement for free public schools was widely supported by the American people. Over the course of his ten-year reign as Secretary of Education, he ignited a contagious spirit of equality whereby progress, for the first time in American history, came to be viewed through the lens of equal access to education for all. Six decades after America declared its Independence, it was the teacher who, at long last, "became the hope of the nation." [86]

With common schools popping up around the country, a call for public high schools soon followed, and by 1851, children in 80 cities across the country were afforded access to a free elementary and high school education. By 1867, the U.S. was home to 116,000 public schools.[87] Ready access to the liberal arts and an emphasis on civic virtue fashioned a new generation of young leaders who desired to make the world a better place. More than anyone else in his era, Mann understood that an education offered Americans a sense of hope; an ability to substitute their fears for dreams.

And he did so by creating a *cordon sanitaire* in the public sphere that allowed reason to reign supreme over passion.

One of the beauties of Mann's movement was that it opened the door for other reform-minded educators to get involved as well. The fight against slavery, as a result, became intertwined with the fight for education. In 1839, the American Statistical Association opened its doors in Mann's hometown of Boston. Its founder was Lemuel Shattuck, a schoolteacher from New England who possessed a firm belief "that the answer to all public questions lay in more facts, more precise facts, and more up-to-date facts." In 1845, Shattuck oversaw the publication of Boston's first census, a groundbreaking document that marshaled in a new era of American statistics and provided the model for the federal government's unprecedented, 640,000-page census of 1850.

In 1857, a North Carolinian named Hilton R. Helper published a book called *Impending Crisis of the South* that used the government's raw census data to show the negative impact that slavery was having on the Southern economy. Although slavery by that point had been abolished in the Northern states for nearly 60 years, moral appeals for the South to do the same were largely ignored.[88] With Helper's book, however, a new fact-based argument was offered for denouncing slavery: the dollar. Dubbed the antebellum era's "most influential antislavery work of nonfiction," Helper's book analyzed the government's census statistics to prove that "the South as a whole, and especially the free white laborer, was being impoverished by slavery." Released at a time when emotions over slavery were at a fever pitch, Helper's cold-blooded, fact-based conclusion that slaveholders were stunting Southern economic progress proved to be a powerful weapon in the anti-slavery cause. In 1860, the Republican Party ordered 100,000 copies to support their nominee, Abraham Lincoln.[89]

* * *

For all the successes of the common school movement, however, they did not come without bitter opposition. By 1847, Horace Mann was exasperated. He had spent the better part of a decade traveling the country on horseback, extolling public schools and promoting equality. Yet regardless of how hard he tried, he could not convince the wealthiest members of society to support his cause. Over time, Mann came to see that businessmen—rather than agreeing to promote the intellectual and moral development of America's next generation—preferred instead to "pursue a course of action by which the godlike powers and capacities of the human soul are wrought into thorough-made products of ignorance and misery and vice." Coal barons, slaveholders, and their ilk were simply unwilling to rid themselves of cheap labor, much less pay for that labor to become educated.

Though he was generally mild-mannered, Mann grew apoplectic over the rich man's aversion to education and loyalty to wealth. He simply could not fathom why individuals with such immense fortune would refuse to help less privileged children obtain an education. "The natural life of an infant," Mann wrote, "should be extinguished as soon as it is born" if her country and its wealthiest citizens refuse to nourish her moral and intellectual capacities. And the wealthy should be deemed "guilty of infanticide."[90]

Two factors in particular contributed to Mann's struggle for free public education, both of which would forecast the attitude of post-Civil War Americans vis-à-vis the merits of liberal education and the pursuit of the common good.

The first was the escalation of religious dogmatism. A committed Unitarian, Mann severely underestimated the degree to which his curriculum—particularly his practice of having teachers read Bible verses to students "without comment" so as to allow students to adopt their own interpretations of Christian morality[91]—would generate "a kind of Unitarian parochial school" that strongly mirrored Mann's own Unitarian beliefs.[92] As a result, he and his cohort of reformers faced considerable objections from Protestants and Catholics alike.

Almost immediately after assuming the role of Secretary, Mann found himself in a struggle with

Protestant evangelicals over the direction of his common school movement. Of particular concern for Protestants was the possibility that students would be subject to sectarian indoctrination. In 1838, Mann was publically attacked by Frederick Packard, Secretary of the American Sunday School Union, for refusing to include a number of the Union's preferred reading books in Massachusetts' school libraries.[93] Though Mann spurned Packard's demands, the conflict would prove portentous. Soon thereafter, evangelicals united in a nationwide push for the teaching of scripture verses in public schools that conformed to their belief that "the Holy Spirit will illumine the mind of the individual as to what God wishes him to understand from the passage which he is reading."[94] The intensive Protestant effort in this regard produced a sort of "religious synthesis" within the common school movement, particularly on the new frontier. From Ohio westward, Protestant missionaries made it their goal to "provide a Protestant paideia for settlers" by granting them access to "the common school, sectarian academies and colleges, Sunday Schools, the pulpit, religious reading," and the like.[95]

Mann's tenure as Secretary also coincided with a massive influx of Irish Catholic immigration. Of the millions who emigrated from Europe to the U.S. in the century after 1820, about a quarter of them came from Ireland.[96] Their arrival sparked an immediate clash with Protestants over the means and ends of Mann's common school movement. In 1844, for instance, Irish Catholics and Protestants engaged in a series of Bible riots in Philadelphia over which version of the Bible should be taught in schools. The riots quickly turned violent, and by July 1844, more than 50 people had been killed.[97] After the riots ended, the Catholics abandoned their efforts to influence the public schools, deciding instead to create their own school system.[98] By 1930, Philadelphia was home to 124 Catholic schools.[99]

The religious battles over common education were incredibly consequential. When Mann first embarked on his project, he had hoped to cultivate a sense of unity across the country—one grounded in a public philosophy of citizenship. At first, political leaders shared Mann's vision. Massachusetts Governor Edward Everett, a Whig, secured necessary funding and helped Mann overcome opposition from religious conservatives like Frederick Packard. When Democrat Marcus Morton replaced Everett the following year, however, he made a concerted effort to abolish the Board of Education and defund the common school movement entirely. Although Morton's efforts ultimately proved unsuccessful, they nevertheless foreshadowed the role that local politicians would play in defining the future of public education.[100]

Marcus Morton was a Jacksonian Democrat—the second source of Mann's frustrations. A Tennessee politician and wealthy plantation owner,* Andrew Jackson capitalized on his fame as a hero in the War of 1812 by running for president in 1824. The electoral votes, however, were split among four candidates, leaving the House to decide America's next president. The House, of course, cast their lot for John Quincy Adams, the immensely qualified secretary of state.

To say that John Quincy Adams was an intellectual would be an understatement. A skilled lawyer who earned a Master of Arts degree from Harvard, Adams spent his younger years immersed in study at mankind's best universities, from Paris to Amsterdam to The Hague. As a Senator, he taught logic at Brown and later became the first professor of Rhetoric and Oratory at Harvard. He also cherished poetry and respected science, serving as the head for many years at the American Academy of Arts and Sciences.

When he became President, Adams adopted a political platform that reflected his deep reverence for knowledge. In his first annual address to Congress, Adams proposed "a national university at Washington, a professional naval academy, a national observatory, a voyage of discovery to the Northwest to follow upon the expedition of Lewis and Clark, an efficient patent office, [and] federal aid to the sciences through a new executive department."[101] Like his parents, John and Abigail, John Quincy firmly believed that the health of

* At the time of his death in 1845, Jackson owned approximately 150 human beings.

American democracy would be forever linked to the education of its citizens.

But alas, Adams "represented a kind of leadership that had outlived its time."[102] After losing the presidential election in 1824, Andrew Jackson—who felt he was owed the presidency for his military accomplishments—launched a crusade to upend the political system. And it was Adams who played the role of foil. As he campaigned around the country, Jackson alleged "bargain and corruption" on the part of Adams and then-House speaker Henry Clay, specifically asserting that Adams had promised to name Clay Secretary of State in exchange for his vote despite the fact that the House had voted in accordance with the Constitution.[103*]

Although he was a powerful slave-owner who had served in politics for decades, Jackson nevertheless billed himself as an "outsider" who would fight for the "common man." The Jacksonian common man, however, was not interested in "philosophy" or similarly haughty matters. Instead he was a restless, commercially-minded yeoman; "to be self-made was his ideal." As Richard Hofstadter wrote, the common man had come to America as "a 'first settler' and created a farm with his ax;" he therefore intended to "let [his]

---

* In fact, it was widely rumored that then-Congressman James Buchanan, a staunch supporter of Jackson, had offered Clay Department of State in exchange for his vote. It is unknown whether Jackson knew of the proposal.

boys do the same." With an entire hemisphere seemingly open for the taking, the commoner raced westward in a "rampant, suspicious, and almost suicidal" quest for monetary gain. [104]

Jackson possessed a cynical, instinctive knack for galvanizing this new breed of American voters. Acutely aware that Adams's "reputation as an intellectual was a red flag," Jackson—a self-described "man of action"—ridiculed the "Indian loving" Adams as "a bookish scholar" who was intent on ending slavery.[105] His anti-intellectualism shtick proved alarmingly effective. Over the course of Jackson's campaign, southern slaveholders and western frontiersmen came to regard the intellectual accomplishments of Adams not as a virtue to be admired but as a vice to be ridiculed. As one group of Jacksonian supporters declared:

> That [Adams] is *learned* we are willing to admit; but his *wisdom* we take leave to question. . . . We confess our attachment to the homely doctrine: thus happily expressed by the great English poet:
>
> > That not to know of things remote
> > From use, obscure and subtle, but to know
> > That which before us lies in daily life
> > Is the prime wisdom.
>
> That wisdom we believe Gen. Jackson

possesses in an eminent degree.[106]

The incumbent Adams failed to win a single southern or western state, leaving Jackson to coast comfortably to the White House. Endowed with a form of "natural wisdom" obtained "straight out of the forest," Jackson came to represent an aberrant species of American intelligence.[107]

As you might expect, Mann's compulsory, sectarian, tax-dependent education movement did not square with this new era of anti-intellectualism, particularly one couched in the rhetoric of westward expansion, religious dogma, and (as we'll see in the next chapter) eastern industrialism. Over the course of the next quarter century, Jackson's supporters grew increasingly more hostile to what they perceived as "the elitist assumptions" of Adams, Mann, and other reformers who advocated in favor of nationwide access to a liberal education. Historian Johann N. Neem, in his book, *Democracy's Schools: The Rise of Public Education in America,* captures this Jacksonian mindset perfectly when he writes, "What role was there for uncommon sense in an era of the common man?"[108]

In the decades leading up to the Civil War, the Jacksonian populists and Protestant evangelicals cemented themselves as leading voices in the battle over the future of American society. Their coalescence proved extremely consequential. As the Jacksonian farmer headed West, he was greeted by Calvinist missionaries who justified his pursuit of material wealth on religious grounds. Back East, the Yankee found himself face-to-face with an unrelenting wave of immigrants, none of whom had any interest in the Yankee's abstract and perhaps disingenuous emphasis on civic virtue. What followed was the eventual cultivation of a new American bourgeois—one characterized by petty-capitalism, proselytized individualism, and aversion to liberal studies. This neoteric culture of "American entrepreneurial radicalism," as Richard Hofstadter described it, would soon come to define American society.[109] Indeed, as America approached the turn of the nineteenth century, the Founders' dream of a country replete with civic-minded, learned citizens was just that—a dream. Instead a new American would lead the country into a new era. His name: the self-made man.

3
THE ENGINEERING OF CONSENT

"The conscious and intelligent manipulation of the organized habits and opinions of the masses is an important element in democratic society. Those who manipulate this unseen mechanism of society constitute an invisible government which is the true ruling power of our country. We are governed, our minds are molded, our tastes formed, and our ideas suggested, largely by men we have never heard of. . . . It is they who pull the wires that control the public mind."

Edward Bernays

For most of the 1800s, the diffusion of wealth and power in the United States was quite broad. Citizens' lives were inherently local, and thus men of moderate means—the preacher, the small merchant, the physician, the journalist, and the lawyer—tended to be held in high regard by their fellow neighbors. This intimacy naturally carried over to the political sphere, where middle-class professionals exerted considerable influence over political decisions.[110] As Henry Adams, writing in the early 1900s, recalled of his hometown New England: "Down to 1850, and even later, New England society was still directed by the professions. Lawyers, physicians, professors, [and] merchants were classes, and acted not as individuals, but as though they were clergymen and each profession were a church."[111]

Localization defined not only politics, but the American economy as well. Steady industrial progress was made in certain pockets of the country, but most Americans worked on farms, transacted in regional markets, and patronized individually owned businesses.[112] As late as 1870, the average number of workers in any given factory was fewer than 10.[113] The concept of scalability had yet to enter into the American mindset, making rapid wealth accumulation nearly impossible for non-gold diggers. Nearly 75 years after the Revolution, there were no more than 20 millionaires in the entire country.[114]

With the onrush of the Industrial Revolution, however, this localized dynamic changed practically overnight. During the half-century following Lincoln's inauguration, the American population exploded from 31 million to 92 million, causing the number of cities with more than 50,000 inhabitants to increase from 16 to 109.[115] As factories and mills sprouted up around the country, natives and immigrants alike flocked to cities in a vigorous pursuit for monetary gain.

Whether American leadership was capable of addressing such a radical transformation was far from clear. Up until that point, the country had been marred in decades of post-Civil War corruption. As Lincoln had predicted, Reconstruction proved to be the most difficult question "ever presented to practical statesmanship."[116] Had Lincoln not gone to the Theatre on Good Friday, perhaps America would have suffered a different fate, for Lincoln's plan of Reconstruction was based on principles of forgiveness and unity. Indeed, against the advice of his compatriots, Lincoln refused to impose political or economic penalties on the South after the War, proposing instead a plan that allowed for full recognition of all confederate states as soon as 10 percent of each state's citizens swore an oath of allegiance to the Union. Lincoln's proposal reflected his heartfelt belief that rehabilitation could be achieved only through reconciliation. "Enough lives have been sacrificed," he wrote. "We must extinguish our resentments if we expect harmony and union."[117]

Destiny, however, had different plans. The plight of Reconstruction was tasked to men who repudiated

Lincoln's harmonious reconstructive proposal.* Rather than coming together in unison, the country embarked on a half-century of confusion and disarray. A dearth of leadership generated an absence of purpose, and from the ashes of disorder grew an unparalleled epoch of political and economic corruption—in the words of historian Richard Write, "corruption suffused government and the economy."[118] Social Darwin liberalism, jim crow conservatism, corporate grafting, rugged individualism, Indian subjugation, and a government brimming with Gilded Age proxies blended together to create a culture of corruption and greed unmatched in American history.

Viewed against the backdrop of the Gilded Age, the Progressive Movement of the early 1900s was, in some sense, America's second democratic Revolution. Like the Founders' uprising, the rise of progressivism had that inexplicable sensation of being both improbable and inevitable. And its leader, of course, was Theodore Roosevelt.

Bedeviled by depression and fearful of decadence, the American populous greeted Roosevelt as a savior. Like John Quincy Adams, Roosevelt was a prolific writer and scholar, publishing some thirty-five books over the course of his lifetime and penning, by some estimates, over 150,000 letters.[119] But like Andrew

* After Lincoln was shot, Confederate Senator Clement C. Clay exclaimed: "God help us. [It] is the worst blow that yet has been struck at the South."

Jackson, Roosevelt was also a military man. After leading the Rough Riders to victory at Kettle Hill during the Spanish-America War, Roosevelt returned home as a national war hero. He then burst onto the political scene with a vigorous combination of intellect and moxie, injecting a spirit of progressivism into the lifeblood of a citizenry that was desperate for leadership.

Culturally speaking, Roosevelt was the country's most influential president in a generation—certainly since Lincoln, and perhaps since Jefferson.[120] His legislative accomplishments were certainly numerous, but more than anything, Roosevelt resurrected the country's perambulatory purpose. Citizenship once again became the country's calling card. Liberty, equality, and the pursuit of the common good displaced corruption, injustice, and the hoarding of private interests. "The prime problem of our nation is to get the right type of good citizenship," Roosevelt declared. And the good citizen:

> will demand liberty for himself, and as a matter of pride he will see to it that others receive liberty which he thus claims as his own. Probably the best test of true love of liberty in any country is the way in which minorities are treated in that country. . . . The gravest wrong upon his country is inflicted by that man,

> whatever his station, who seeks to make his countrymen divide primarily in the line that separated class from class, occupation from occupation, men of more wealth from men of less wealth, instead of remembering that the only safe standard is that which judges each man on his worth as a man, whether he be rich or whether he be poor, without regard to his profession or to his station in life. Such is the only true democratic test, the only test that can with propriety be applied in a republic.[121]

For Roosevelt, the Bully pulpit served as a tool of Socratic persuasion. He used the awesome power of the presidency to implore his fellow citizens to seek the common good and rise above the material preoccupations that threated to distract them from higher ends. "If there is one thing which we should wish as a Nation to avoid," Roosevelt cautioned, "it is the teaching of those who would reenforce the lower promptings of our hearts, and so teach us to seek only a life of effortless ease, of mere material comfort."[122]

Roosevelt thus did his best to prevent America from descending upon the gates of Dante's Fourth Circle. Under his leadership, the government acted as a vigilant mediator for the security and prosperity of all citizens. In 1906 alone, the Roosevelt administration created the Department of Labor and oversaw the passing of several progressive legislative enactments, including the Pure Food and Drug Act, the Meat Inspection Act, the Hepburn Railway Rate Act, and the Naturalization Act. In stark contrast to today, it was the government—not private industry—that protected citizens from exploitation and unfair treatment.

Roosevelt's emphasis on civic duty transformed the common man into the public citizen. And because the public citizen is naturally concerned first and foremost with education, one of the major benefactors of the Roosevelt era was the American student. In 1900, only 50 percent of American children attended school on a daily basis, including only 31 percent of African Americans and other minorities. By 1910, 60 percent of all children were in school, including 45 percent of minorities. And by 1920, those numbers had grown to 64 percent and 54 percent, respectively.[123]

Lurking in the shadows of progress, however, was an American appetite for profit that even Roosevelt could not fully comprehend. For the first time in world history, the prospect of colossal wealth was available to the masses. And for many Americans, that prospect was simply irresistible—an attitude that Mark Twain captured in the form of Colonel Beriah Sellers, one of the characters in *The Gilded Age: A Tale of Today*. After concocting "the Medical Wonder of the Age!"—a fanciful ointment he calls Beriah Sellers' Infallible Imperial Oriental Optic Liniment and Salvation for Sore

Eyes—Sellers decides to travel from small-town America to New York City in order to bring his idea to market. His creation lacks a crucial ingredient, but that doesn't stop him; the prospect of securing fabulous wealth is simply too enticing to ignore: "Annual income—well, God only knows how many millions and millions apiece!"[124]

Though Roosevelt had succeeded in creating a culture that prioritized the common good over the material good, history reveals that the transformation was ultimately fleeting. Indeed, one of the first signs of America's changing culture was its shift in vernacular. Prior to the Industrial Revolution, the word "shop," for example, was used as a noun; people walked "to the shop," perhaps to buy a cucumber or a sweater. But in the twentieth century, "shop" became a verb; urbanites started to "go shopping" without any particular reason for doing so other than to see what caught their eye.

The department store, in this sense, was revolutionary. As the novelist Émile Zola wrote from France, the Macy's of the Industrial Age "democratized luxury." One no longer needed to be wealthy in order to view lavish articles of clothing, jewelry, and the like. Instead everyone was presumed a customer. Goods were marketed for mass appeal and department stores offered their services *carte blanche* to the general public: free delivery, free returns, and credit accounts for all.[125] As William Leach writes, the department store introduced a new kind of "commercial aesthetic" to

America. Hotels, amusement parks, and chain stores soon began to adopt the Wanamaker model of affluence. This sudden accentuation of luxury terrified Theodore Roosevelt, who instinctively discerned luxury's power to corrupt the soul of the citizen. "Material development means nothing to a nation as an end in itself," the president avowed in 1907. "If America is to stand simply for the accumulation of what tells for comfort and luxury, then it will stand for little indeed when looked at through the vistas of the ages."[126]

Roosevelt's warning did not scare corporate America, however. As the economist Thorstein Veblen wrote in the early twentieth century, the corporation had by 1900 "come not only to dominate the economic structure but to be the master institution of civilized life."[127] Businessmen, in turn, began to see that survival in America's consumption community rested in large part on their ability to foster brand loyalty. What followed was an Industrial Age advertising boom that was nothing short of spectacular. As of 1867, American businesses spent roughly $50 million per year on advertising; by 1900, spending had increased tenfold to $500 million; and by 1950 it had reached $5.5 billion.[128]

The steady flow of immigrants and the continual migration of Americans to cities created an identity crisis of sorts for those who lacked physical ties to their new communities. "We are unsettled to the very roots of our being," wrote a twenty-five-year-old Walter Lippmann in 1914. "We have changed our environment more quickly than we know how to change ourselves."[129] Intuiting this void, businesses began to create their own distinctive communities of like-minded consumers. The brisk proliferation of advertising outlets—radio, newspapers, billboards, magazines, theme parks, and department stores—offered businesses coast-to-coast access to an unprecedented number of customers. Americans from all walks of life could "Walk a Mile with Camel" or quench their thirst in style with a nice cold bottle of Coca-Cola, "the glass of fashion."[130] As historian Daniel Boorstin emphasizes, this method of advertising was both scientifically designed and deliberately executed; it was not simply another form of salesmanship: "While the salesman persuaded the customer that [an] item was peculiarly suited to his unique needs, the advertisement persuaded *groups* of buyers that the item was well suited to the needs of all persons in the group. The advertisement succeeded when it discovered, defined, and persuaded a new community of consumers."[131]

The most consequential voice in the American marketing movement was that of Edward Bernays. A nephew twice over of Sigmund Freud, Bernays was hired by the Committee on Public Information during World War I to build domestic and foreign support for America's war efforts, particularly in Latin America. It was in this capacity that he learned the power of propaganda, or, as he described it, "psychological warfare."[132]

Fascinated by the effectiveness of propaganda during the War, Bernays set out to determine whether the same techniques might prove equally effective during peacetime. Drawing on the insights of his Uncle Sigmund, he developed an approach to advertising called "the engineering of consent." In his eponymously named work, *Propaganda,* Bernays explained that his method of persuasion allows propagandists like himself to "control and regiment the masses according to our will without [the consumer] knowing about it." To effectively execute this approach, an advertiser must direct his messaging to the irrational, unconscious part of the consumer's malleable mind. This is because, for Bernays, the consumer's decision to act is not the product of reasoned judgment but rather the outgrowth of "a mélange of impressions stamped on his mind by outside influences which unconsciously control his thought." For example, "a man buying a car may think he wants it for purposes of locomotion," but in fact he "want[s] it because it is a symbol of social position, an evidence of his success in business, or a means of pleasing his wife."[133]

The effectiveness of Bernays's psychological approach to advertising was both immediate and profound. Just weeks before the 1924 presidential election, Bernays was hired by President Calvin Coolidge's campaign to counteract the president's dour public image.* With deliberate speed, Bernays arranged for dozens of Broadway's biggest stars to board a train from New York to Washington, where Coolidge awaited them for a breakfast of pancakes and sausages. Afterward, the crowd shuffled out to the White House lawn, where Al Jolson treated them to a rousing new hit, "Keep Coolidge." The next day, the *New York Times* published a front-page picture of a jolly Coolidge, laughing and smiling with his new friends, along with the byline, "Actors Eat Cakes with the Coolidges . . . President Nearly Laughs." Coolidge would go on to win the 1924 election by a popular vote margin of 25.2 percent, which to this day remains one of the most dominant victories in American history.[134] Reflecting on Coolidge's success four years later, Bernays wrote: "Political campaigns today are all side shows, all honors, all bombast, glitter, and speeches. These are for the most part unrelated to the main business of studying the party scientifically, of supplying the public with party, candidate, platform, and performance, and selling the public these ideas and products."[135] Over the course of the next several decades, Bernays would use these lessons to craft the public images of Presidents Wilson, Hoover, and Eisenhower.[136]

Bernays's efforts in private industry were equally impactful. Though he worked for a litany of

* An oft-repeated story tells of a young woman, sitting a dinner party with Coolidge, who bet that she could make the president say three words. "You lose," said Coolidge, without looking up.

corporations—General Electric, Procter & Gamble, and CBS among them—it was his work for the American Tobacco Company for which he is most often remembered. In 1929, the President of American Tobacco, George Washington Hill, called on Bernays to implement a more aggressive advertising campaign for soliciting women smokers. At the time, women consumed only twelve percent of all cigarettes sold.[137] As Bernays recounted, "Hill called me in. 'How can we get women to smoke in the street?' They're smoking indoors. But damn it, if they spend half the time outdoors and we can't get 'em to smoke outdoors, we'll damn near double our female market. Do something. Act!"

As Allan Brandt describes in his book, *The Cigarette Century*, Bernays took Hill's marching orders and set out to "identify and destroy the taboos associated with public smoking for women." To that end, Bernays called upon New York psychoanalyst and Freudian disciple A. A. Brill. "Today the emancipation of women has suppressed many of their feminine desires," Brill told Bernays. "More women now do the same work as men do. Many women bear no children; those who do bear fewer children. Feminine traits are masked. Cigarettes, which are equated with men, become torches with freedom."

Promptly grasping the propaganda power inherent in Brill's "torches with freedom" remark, Bernays "called up a young debutante friend of mine and I said, 'would you be willing to ask some of your debutante friends and obviously the young men to walk in the [1929 New York City Easter Parade] lighting torches of freedom as a protest against men's inhumanity to women?'" "Well obviously," Bernays sniped, "the young woman snapped it up." The slogan caught fire instantly. Prior to the march, feminist leader Ruth Hale passed out invitations that read: "Women! Light another torch of freedom! Fight another sex taboo!"

On Easter Sunday, onlookers gathered to watch the women march through Midtown Manhattan puffing their Lucky Strikes. The following day, the *New York Times* published front-page photographs of women smoking their torches of freedom. Within five weeks, private smoking rooms throughout New York opened to women for the first time.[138] And by 1935, the number of women smoking cigarettes had nearly doubled.[139] Bernays, reflecting years later on the success of his secret marketing crusade, wrote: "Age-old customs, I learned, could be broken down by a dramatic appeal, disseminated by the network of media."[140]

The ultimate implementation of Bernays's psychological propaganda techniques came during World War II, though not on America's behalf. As the German killing machine moved westward, President Franklin Roosevelt knew that it was only a matter of time before America would have to intervene. In contemplating how to best cultivate public support for intervention, FDR considered reaching out to Bernays.

The president ultimately opted against the idea, however, after Supreme Court Justice Felix Frankfurter wrote him a letter lambasting Bernays and others like him as "professional poisoners of the public mind, exploiters of foolishness, fanaticism, and self-interest."[141]

But Bernays's influence would be felt nonetheless. Joseph Goebbels, who served as Reich Minister of Propaganda from 1933 to 1945, was an avid admirer of Bernays's work (his Jewish ancestry notwithstanding). Having surely read *Mein Kampf*, Goebbels learned from Hitler that the "broad masses of a nation are always more easily corrupted in the deeper strata of their emotional nature than consciously or voluntarily."[142] Beynays's psychological formula, therefore, was tailor-made to fulfill Hitler's vision.

Utilizing Bernays's book, *Crystallizing Public Opinion*, Goebbels created a "*führer* cult" around Adolf Hitler by adopting the slogan, *Ein Volk, ein Reich, ein Führer* (One People, One Empire, One Leader).[143] The slogan—which reflected the *führer*'s desire to create the *Volksgemeinschaft*, an ideal society occupied by pure Germans only—appeared on countless posters and in numerous publications around the world. Its effectiveness was terrifying. In an April 1940 meeting between William Stephenson, the head of the British Security Coordination, and President Roosevelt, Stephenson told the president that it would take Hitler little time to subjugate the masses of America. "The *führer* is not just a lunatic," Stephenson said. "He's an evil genius. The weapons in his armory are like nothing in history. His propaganda is sophisticated. His control of the people is technologically clever. He has torn up the military textbooks and written his own. His strategy is to spread terror, fear, and mutual suspicion."[144] Stephenson's concerns were justified. Just a few months before Stephenson met with FDR, 20,000 Americans had descended upon New York City to euphorically express their support for the Nazi cause. A decade after Bernays arranged to have feminists puff Lucky Strikes down Fifth Avenue, his model of psychological warfare was being used to cultivate a cult of Nazi supporters at Madison Square Garden.

History, of course, rhymes. In 2017, American venture capitalist Roger McNamee, who made a fortune as an early investor in Facebook, left the company after he discovered that Mark Zuckerberg had adopted Bernays's psy-ops methods to keep users addicted to his platform. "They have taken all the techniques of Edward Bernays and Joseph Goebbels," McNamee said, "and they've mapped it onto an all-day product with highly personalized information to addict you." It is "a persuasion engine unlike any created in history."[145]

* * *

The overlap between Bernays's style of advertising in capitalist America and Hitler's model of governance in Nazi Germany was not fortuitous happenstance. To be sure, some of America's most influential businessmen provided direct assistance to the Third Reich. Fred Koch—the father of the "Koch Brothers," Charles and David, who oversee the furtive network of dark money donors funding today's Republican Party—earned a significant portion of his post-Depression fortune by contracting with Hitler to build the third largest oil refinery in Germany. As Jane Mayer details in her book *Dark Money*, Fred Koch's refinery, which was finished in 1935, was "a key component of the Nazi war machine," as it produced the high-octane fuel necessary to execute bombing raids over cities like Coventry. An avaricious child of the Industrial Age, Fred Koch preferred the virtues of fascism and its nurturing of diligent, hard-working citizens over America's "nascent welfare state" and its fostering of indolent factory workers. Writing to a friend in 1938, Koch confessed:

> I am of the opinion that the only sound countries in the world are Germany, Italy, and Japan, simply because they are all working and working hard. The laboring people in those countries are proportionately much better off than they are any place else in the world. When you contrast the state of mind of Germany today with what it was in 1925 you begin to think that perhaps this

> course of idleness, feeding at the public trough, dependence on government, etc., with which we are afflicted is not permanent and can be overcome.[146*]

Koch was not the only American to strike a Faustian bargain with the Nazis. From the moment Hitler came to power, the Nazi party adopted as one of its central missions the identification and elimination of Germany's 600,000 Jews from the face of the Earth. And by "Jews," Hitler did not mean those who merely practiced Judaism; to the contrary, he intended to hunt down "those of Jewish blood, regardless of their assimilation, intermarriage, religious activity, or even conversion to Christianity." Logistically speaking, this was a complex task, and of course no computer existed. Hitler thus turned to IBM's subsidiary in Germany, "Dehomag," which at the time was the world's leader in census operations. Hitler knew that Dehomag, through its punch card and card sorting system, had the ability to both count and locate the Jews on a mass scale. So in 1933, he struck a deal with IBM to receive more than

---

* Fred Koch was so enamored with German citizens' work ethic that he employed a German governess to care for his first two sons, Freddie and Charles. "A fervent Nazi sympathizer," the nanny "frequently touted Hitler's virtues" and "enforced a rigid toilet-training regimen requiring the boys to produce morning bowel movements precisely on schedule or be force-fed castor oil and subjected to enemas." Her love of the Koch boys did not supplant her love of Hitler, however. After Germany invaded France, the nanny returned to her homeland "to join the *führer* in celebration."

2,000 card-sorting machines, which in turn were set up at every major concentration camp across Europe. Via these automated tools of human destruction, the Jews were rounded up and sent off to die with "icy precession." Back in New York, the personal representatives to IBM chairman, Thomas Watson, kept in "constant contract" with Berlin, "monitoring activities" so as to ensure "that the parent company . . . was not cut out of any of the profits or business opportunities Nazism presented." And when Congress passed a law making direct contact with Germany illegal, "IBM's Swiss office became the nexus, providing the New York office continuous information and credible deniability."[147]

Businessmen like Koch and Watson were not anomalous; they personified the bludgeoning political economy that had taken hold of American society after the Great Depression. The philosophy underlying this new political economy was, by and large, amoral; it was indifferent to virtue and hospitable to the consumption of wealth.[148] It therefore stood in a sharp contrast to the progressive philosophies of Teddy Roosevelt and Woodrow Wilson, both of whom advocated for a political economy of citizenship. Indeed, Roosevelt and Wilson conducted themselves in the spirit of the Federalists and Anti-Federalists—although they endorsed different means, they sought the same end.

Prior to 1920, economic arguments retained a cadence of citizenship that focused primarily on whether a particular policy would "promote or erode the moral qualities self-government requires." Roosevelt, for example, felt that a national, centralized federal government offered the best means of controlling the ever-expanding industrial landscape. He therefore sought to consolidate power and fight big business with big government. But in seeking to persuade America on the merits of his argument, he spoke primarily in terms of upholding virtue. "Material well-being is a great good," Roosevelt wrote in 1910, "but it is a great good chiefly as a means for the upbuilding upon it of a high and fine type of character, private and public."[149]

Wilson, in contrast to Roosevelt, feared "the curse of bigness." He sought to regulate competition by decentralizing the economy and reintroducing "small-scale, self-sufficient, 'free American communities'" to the economic sphere. But he too prioritized a virtuous citizenry. He hoped to guide the country into an age where citizens might "look[] about their neighbors, finding credit according to their character, not according to their connections."[150]

Both men—as Harvard professor and political philosopher Michael Sandel explains in his work, *Democracy's Discontent*—were equally concerned "about the sort of citizens the economic arrangements of their day were likely to *produce*" (emphasis mine). For Roosevelt and Wilson, it was production, not consumption, that defined the relationship between citizens and their government. During the Progressive era, Americans assumed an identity that reflected their productive role in society—as farmers or artisans, teachers or lawyers, industrial workers or shop owners.[151]

But beginning in the 1920s, the nation's thought leaders began to supplant the civic-minded, production-oriented philosophies of Roosevelt and Wilson with the capitalist-minded, consumer-oriented philosophies of Warren Harding and Calvin Coolidge. "This is essentially a business country," President Harding declared in 1920. Coolidge, Harding's Vice President and eventual successor, agreed: "After all, the chief business of the American people is business. They are profoundly concerned with producing, buying, selling, investing and prospering in the world. I am strongly of opinion that the great majority of people will always find these are moving impulses of our life."[152] In this new land of desire, citizens were affiliated less by what they *contributed* to society than by what they *took* from society; less by the *knowledge* they acquired than by the *goods* they acquired. And as whole, society's focus was on having rather than being; on prices rather than wages; and on personal repute rather than communal improvement.

By the time Harry Truman replaced FDR in 1945, the Coolidge consumerism model had become enshrined in law. The groundswell for this legal transformation began seven years earlier, in 1938, when

Franklin Roosevelt appointed a Yale professor by the name of Thurman Arnold to head the Antitrust Division of the Justice Department. The purpose of the Antitrust Division, of course, is revealed in its name—it is, quite literally, an *anti-trust* branch of the government. As Senator John Sherman, the namesake of the 1890 Sherman Antitrust Act, explained at the time of its passing: "The concentrated power of the trust amounted to 'a kingly prerogative, inconsistent with our form of government, and should be subject to the strong resistance of the State and national authorities. . . . If we will not endure a king as a political power we should not endure a king over the production, transportation, and sale of any of the necessities of life.'" The Antitrust arm of the Justice Department was therefore created "to protect the consumer from monopoly pricing and to preserve the decentralized economy of small businesses and trades long seen as essential to self-government."[153]

Prior to the Progressive era, antitrust law was a vehicle seldom used by the government. But under the leadership of Presidents Roosevelt and Wilson, antitrust assumed an important role in shaping the tenor of America's economic philosophy. The cases brought on behalf of the government reflected the Progressive viewpoint noted above—one that sought to preserve competitiveness among all market participants by assessing economic equality from the perspective of the producer rather than the consumer. Louis Brandeis, the unofficial antitrust spokesmen during the Progressive years, staunchly defended this approach. For he believed that if the focus of antitrust law were on ensuring price competition rather than on safeguarding small, independent producers, then the virtues of citizenship would be lost. Like Bernays, Brandeis shrewdly intuited the impact that advertising had on rational judgment. Concerned only with price, Brandeis regarded the "thoughtless" consumer as "servile, indulgent, indolent, ignorant," and "easily manipulated by advertising."[154] To link the wagon of law to the horse of the consumer would, in Brandeis's view, result in the consumer becoming an "instrument of monopoly."

Thurman Arnold, however, ridiculed the "old religion" of Brandeis and the Progressives. Antitrust law, for Arnold, was concerned above all with the consumer: "there is only one sensible test which we can apply to the privilege of [a large] organization: Does it increase the *efficiency* of production or distribution and pass the *savings* on to consumers?" (emphasis mine). As Professor Sandel explains in his fantastic exposition of American antitrust law, Arnold "was the first major antitrust advocate to reject altogether the civic argument for antitrust and to insist exclusively on the consumerist one." And his influence was tremendous. By the time he left the Justice Department in 1943, he had filed and won more antitrust cases than had been initiated in the entire half-century prior to his appointment. In less than a decade, the Antitrust

Division had morphed from a civic-oriented department to a consumer-oriented department. And although it may not have been apparent at the time, this ethical transformation "intimated a broader change in the way Americans would think about economics and politics through the rest of the century."[155]

By the time Ralph Nader rocked the automobile industry in 1965 with his book, *Unsafe at Any Speed,* the Arnold model of consumerism had become mainstream. In exposing car manufacturers' conscious decisions to prioritize financial gain over driver safety—a revelation that prompted Congress to create the National Highway Traffic Safety Administration—Nader fundamentally concerned himself with "citizen-consumers." For him, the "modern wisdom" of antitrust law was its impact on "the *prices* people pay for their bread, gasoline, auto parts, prescription drugs, and houses" (emphasis mine).[156]

The steady rationalization of consumerism took hold of America in the early 1900s. By mid-century, it was the dominant economic ideology. From this vantage point, it can be seen that businessmen like Fred Koch embodied a new American spirit of individual and economic growth. Nazism was perhaps objectionable, but, to them, it was not immoral.

* * *

It is impossible to overstate the impact that

Bernays's psychological methods of manipulation, coupled with the post-Great Depression emphasis on consumerism, had on American culture. As we know from Plato, civilization begins its decline once self-love becomes its prevailing credo. Adam Smith, thirty years before the Constitution was ratified, addressed this very principle in *A Theory of Moral Sentiments* when he wrote that "[c]arelessness and lack of economy are universally disapproved of, . . . not as proceeding from a want of benevolence but from a want of proper attention to the objects of self-interest."[157] de Tocqueville reiterated the same proposition in *Democracy in America* when he forewarned that the ultimate success of democracy depended in large part on getting "self-interest rightly understood." Prior to the Civil War, the process of getting self-interest rightly understood was achieved through the aforementioned means of persuasion advocated by John Quincy Adams—i.e., where persuaders operated by proof rather than by influence and sought justice rather than utility.

But with the advent of scientifically orchestrated marketing campaigns and legal justifications for consumerism, the Adams model of persuasion slowly became inverted. Persuaders began to operate by influence rather than by proof and arguments started to drift away from justice and toward utility. In due time, freedom of choice began to imply freedom to purchase, individual fulfillment began to take precedence over communal advancement, and the country as a whole gradually moved away from the belief that happiness was rooted in the pursuit of the common good. Self-interest, as a result, became synonymous with self-love.

Nowhere was this shift more palpable than in the self-help phenomenon of Dale Carnegie. Born on a Missouri farm as Dale "Carnagey" in 1888, he later changed his last name to "Carnegie" to capitalize on the fame of the great oil tycoon, Andrew Carnegie.[158] From his early days, Dale Carnegie desired to be a public speaker. His idol was William Jennings Bryan, the famed orator who traveled the Chautauqua lecture circuit and later served as the mouthpiece of the anti-evolution movement.[159*]

In 1912, the 34-year-old Carnegie moved to New York City, where he decided to teach a public speaking course at a local YMCA. It was there he noticed that his "students," most of whom were salesmen, lacked the courage necessary to make a sales pitch to a stranger. Carnegie thus devised a set of techniques intended to

---

* The capstone of Bryan's career came during the infamous Scopes Trial in 1925. Hired by the World Christian Fundamentals Association to defend state laws banning the teaching of evolution in public schools, Bryan made the mistake of subjecting himself to cross-examination by renowned trial lawyer Clarence Darrow, who proceeded to question Bryan on his views of the Bible: "Asked when the Flood occurred, Bryan consulted Ussher's Bible Concordance, and gave the date as 2348 BC, or 4,273 years ago. Did not Bryan know, asked Darrow, that Chinese civilization had been traced back at least 7,000 years? Bryan conceded that he did not. When he was asked if the records of any other religion made mention of a flood at the time he cited, Bryan replied: 'The Christian religion has always been good enough for me—I never found it necessary to study any competing religion.'"

help the salesmen "conquer fear." His methods worked. Before long, Carnegie was traveling the country holding public speaking workshops that were open to aspiring capitalists for a fee. His "textbook," *How to Win Friends and Influence People*, hit the market in 1936 and was an instant bestseller. During the first two years after its publication, it sold 5,000 copies *per day*. It remained on the bestseller list for an entire decade and as of today has sold more than 30 million copies.[160]

Carnegie's insights were both intellectually regressive and psychologically incisive. By implementing Freudian principles of desire into his salesmanship routine, he figured out that "[t]he only way I can get you to do anything is by giving you what you want." And what you want is "the desire to be important."[161] Carnegie's guidance accordingly taught capitalists how to manipulate other people's emotional tendencies in order to make them act on their consumer impulses. The exercise itself was fundamentally anti-rational. Drawing on the lessons of Al Capone and John Wanamaker, Carnegie came to believe that "criticism is dangerous, because it wounds a person's precious pride, hurts his sense of importance, and arouses resentment." Thus there was no point in rational discourse because, as Wanamaker said, "God has not seen fit to distribute evenly the gift of intelligence."[162] As such, Carnegie's emphasis was on personality rather than character and on perception rather than reflection. "The only way to get the best of an argument is to avoid it." "Smile" because it is "A Simple Way to make a Good First Impression." "Keep your human contacts smooth and pleasant." "Encourage others to talk about themselves." In Carnegie's view, words were nothing more than slogans; nuance, context, or any other form of specificity that might shed light on the precise origin an idea was pruned away in the interest of "straight talk."[163]

Carnegie perfected his method of persuasion at a time when Americans were desperate for a new formula of success—one that would allow them to unlock the chains of despair that had whitewashed the American economy during the Great Depression. When his book was published in 1936, American unemployment stood at a daunting 16.9 percent.[164] Carnegie earnestly and admirably hoped that by creating a culture of positive employer-employee relations, the country would be able to shed the sentiment of hopelessness that had permeated the public sphere. And for a society marred by pessimism, Carnegie's particular brand of optimism was both refreshing and useful.

But despite Carnegie's laudable aims—indeed we should heed his call to purge hostility from contemporary discourse—his theory of persuasion simply does not allow for rational dialogue once put into practice. In fact it encourages egotism; his thesis is that you don't *make* friends, you *win* them. And you win them via *influence,* not proof—literally the inverse of

Adams's persuasive technique. Carnegie's approach creates an ethical dilemma that pins hypocrisy against sincerity and success against knowledge. "See, Biff," Happy Loman tells his brother in *Death of a Salesman*, "everybody around me is so false that I'm constantly lowering my ideals. . ."[165] Indeed almost every "lesson" in Carnegie's book rests on the premise that people are driven by vanity and self-interest, flaws that Carnegie's students can then manipulate to their own advantage. In terms of fulfilling the Founders' goal of a virtuous republic, Carnegie's approach is infinitely regressive. As Richard Huber writes in *The American Idea of Success*: "What happens to moral honesty when people become objects, when relationships are stained by the need to sell, when the self is soiled by the demand to sell the self?"[166]

Carnegie's self-help blueprint represented a sharp divergence from the Revolutionary model of self-improvement. Benjamin Franklin, arguably the forefather of the self-help genre, devised a list of 13 "virtues" intended to guide ambitious entrepreneurs in their quest for success: "Use no hurtful deceit. Think innocently and justly; and if you speak, speak accordingly." "Resolve to perform what you *ought*." "Avoid trifling conversation." "Be always employed in something useful."[167] For Franklin, there was a civic *unity* between thought and action.

Horatio Alger, writing in the latter half of the nineteenth century, echoed Franklin's call for virtue. In

1868, he published *Ragged Dick,* the first novel to adopt what would later become known as the Horatio Alger formula of self-improvement. Ragged Dick emerges from destitution into a well-deserved fortune, but he does so by exhibiting the traditional traits of virtue—industry, frugality, a penchant for self-improvement—"which set him apart from the ne'er-do-wells and confidence men who populate his adventures in the streets of New York."[168]

Carnegie's personality guide, however, was not written in the virtuous tradition of Franklin or Alger. I would posit instead that Carnegie's philosophy pushes human beings toward what Ralph Waldo Emerson degradingly characterized as a "mere thinker"—one who waltzes through life focused on his task but ignorant of his purpose. In the right state, Emerson says, Man is "*Man Thinking.*" His function is to "cheer, to raise, and to guide men by showing them facts amidst appearances." But a "mere thinker" is just the opposite; he may be a molder of opinions but he is not a cultivator of knowledge. "Man hopes," Emerson says. But "Genius creates." *Man Thinking* seeks knowledge through reason and observation, whereas a mere thinker is a "parrot of other men's thinking."[169]

A "Bernagie thinker," if you will (Bernays + Carnegie), is a more modern version of Emerson's mere thinker. He not only parrots other men's thinking; he *manipulates* other men's thinking for his own material purposes. The Bernagie thinker slithers his way through society shunning self-reflection in favor of self-absorption and fomenting irrationality at the expense of critical thinking; the propagandists "pull the wires that control the public mind" while the crowd-pleasers "smile" as they seek to cozy favor with our "pride and vanity."[170]

In many ways it was the Bernagie thinker whom Dr. Martin Luther King, Jr., had in mind while sitting "alone for days in the dull monotony of a narrow jail cell" in Alabama. Addressing the eight white clergymen who had "been *influenced* by the argument of outsiders coming" into Birmingham to protest jim crow segregation (emphasis mine), Dr. King wrote that he had "almost reached the regrettable conclusion that the Negro's great stumbling block in the stride toward freedom is not the White Citizens Councillor or the Ku Klux Klanner but the white moderate who is more devoted to order than to justice; who prefers a negative peace which is the absence of tension to a positive peace which is the presence of justice. . . ." Herein lies the very purpose of Dr. King's nonviolence movement—to create a tension between *Man Thinking,* who "recognized the urgency of the moment and sensed the need . . . to combat the disease of segregation," and the mere thinker, who had "unconsciously become insensitive to the problems of the masses." In prose that can only be described as lyrical, Dr. King explained why his philosophy of nonviolence was necessary to bridge the gap between racism and enlightenment: "Just as

Socrates felt that it was necessary to create a tension in the mind so that individuals could rise from the bondage of myths and half-truths to the unfettered realm of creative analysis and objective appraisal, we must see the need of having nonviolent gadflies to create the kind of tension in society that will help men to rise from the dark depths of prejudice and racism to the majestic heights of understanding and brotherhood."[171] Had Dr. King read *How to Win Friends and Influence People* rather than the *Apology*, perhaps he wouldn't have been shot; but perhaps we would still be living in a country defined by law as separate but equal.

* * *

The Bernagie phenomenon was not incidental. It reflected the education (or lack thereof) that students were receiving in public schools—a tragedy that manifested itself all too fully in the story of Dr. Harold Rugg, one of the most renowned educators in American history. In the 1920s and 1930s, Rugg—then a professor at Columbia University's Teachers College—created a series of textbooks that challenged the morality of consumerism and taught students to be skeptical of advertising. Like Thomas Jefferson and Horace Mann, Rugg "focused on citizenship education;" he believed that an American education should imbue students with the tools necessary to become engaged and active citizens in American society.[172]

Rugg's decision to create his own educational curriculum stemmed from his belief that students were terribly ill-equipped to deal with the rise and consequences of industrial society. In the early 1920s, he was asked by the National Society for the Study of Education to conduct a systematic review of the social studies curricula that was in place at public schools around the country. His findings were published in 1923 in his work, *The Social Studies in the Elementary and Secondary School,* which begins with the following question: "Do the Social Studies Prepare Pupils Adequately for Life Activities?" Resolving that, no, "they do not," Rugg explained that most students rarely engaged in thoughtful deliberation about political and social matters. In particular, he found that "impulse" rather than "critical judgment" formed "the basis upon which our social and political decisions are made," and that the public school curricula failed to provide students with "knowledge about the issues of contemporary life and how . . . to act intelligently upon them."

Of particular concern for Rugg was the emphasis that schools placed on the rote memorization of inconsequential facts, an approach to learning that he deemed both dull and impractical. "The schools are following the path of least resistance . . . based upon 'no theories at all,'" he wrote. "The practice implicitly assumes . . . that clear thinking and right conduct will issue from the mere acquiring of information."[173] For

Rugg, it was critical that "young people . . . [be able to] confront the alternatives set out before them. How else can human beings practice decision making than by confronting issues?"[174] In other words, students must be taught to examine the *consequences* that facts generate, not just the facts themselves.

In 1928 (incidentally, the same year Bernays published *Propaganda*), Rugg proposed his own innovative social studies curriculum that combined the traditional subjects of history, geography, and civics with an increased focus on "current problems such as the corporate economy, agricultural depression, unequal distribution of wealth, the need for economic planning, intercultural relations and international cooperation." Rugg's textbooks additionally emphasized "the important role of advertising and business in determining the content of newspapers and magazines." One textbook (published in 1931) stated:

> We have seen the widespread tendency for tabloid picture newspapers and other sensational periodicals to print 'news' without too great regard for accuracy. Hence, although reputable publishers are already doing much to improve the character of the press, insistent problems present themselves. Underlying them are difficult questions of propaganda and censorship. Similarly, there emerge the

> equally important problems of the more fundamental education of our people, of the cultivation of a taste for better literature and of a demand for a more scientific attitude in the press.[175]

For the better part of the 1930s, Rugg's textbooks—which were sold to elementary, middle school, and high school students alike—were among the most popular in the country. As Rugg biographer Ronald Evans writes, "Rugg created an avant-garde social studies program, a prototype for a unified, interdisciplinary curriculum focused on issues and problems and aimed at education for social justice."[176] From 1929-1939, Rugg's textbooks provided a Jeffersonian education to more than 3 million American students across 4,200 school districts.[177] In the minds of local educators, they were the most "complete textbooks dealing with social science available on the American market."[178]

With the benefit of context, it is not difficult to see why. At the time Rugg's textbooks were in circulation, the country was recovering from one world war and on the cusp of another. Rugg's textbooks, unlike others of the era, grappled with the dangers of authoritarianism. Rather than peddling vacuous patriotism and painting a fictitious portrait of history, Rugg wanted students to recognize that the United States was not immune from tyranny. He knew, like H.G. Wells, that "civilization is in a race between education and catastrophe." Healthy skepticism, particularly of big business and its influence on government, was essential if America wanted to avoid the fate of Europe. As Robert Evans elegantly writes, Rugg "placed a higher value on human rights than on private property, wanted students to wrestle with the issues raised by the dilemmas of capitalism, and wanted schools to teach about the social world, past and present, as if people mattered."[179]

In 1939, however, Rugg's liberal philosophy ignited a reaction from corporate America that can only be described as hysteria. That year, the American Federation of Advertising (AFA) joined forces with the National Association of Manufacturers (NAM) to launch "a large campaign to rid schools of Communist-infiltrated school texts and, in particular, to purge schools of Rugg's work." Norman S. Rose, the president of the AFA and the advertising manager at the *Christian Science Monitor*, gave a speech in 1940 at New York's World Fair in which he railed against the use of Rugg's "subversive" textbooks, declaring: "Textbooks used by thousands of American school children attacked American business, American advertising, [and] time-tried and time-honored American ways of living and prospering." Alfred T. Falk, the Director of AFA's Bureau of Research and Education, similarly "expressed great concern about [Rugg's] ability to indoctrinate students with propaganda against advertising."[180] In 1940, *Nation's Business* entered the controversy with an attack on the "anti-advertising" material that had been "planted" in Rugg's social science textbooks. The editors (accurately, though not approvingly) characterized Rugg's textbooks as teaching students that "advertising is an economic waste, that a high proportion of advertising is dishonest, and that advertised products are pretty likely to be untrustworthy."[181] *Forbes* magazine founder, B.C. Forbes, likewise used his platform to denounce Rugg's "treacherous teachings."[182]

On November 14, 1940, in an address before three thousand leaders of the American Petroleum Institute, NAM President H. W. Prentis, Jr., charged that "creeping collectivism" had invaded the public schools via social science textbooks that undermined children's faith in the free enterprise system. At the time, NAM was engaged in a frantic effort to rehabilitate a public image that had been destroyed in the market crash and defamed by the New Deal. Its propaganda apparatus was massive, with half of its budget—some $800,000—devoted to what Bernays called "public relations."[183] Signaling out Rugg's work in particular, Prentis called on "every patriotic American citizen . . . to insist that if collectivist doctrines are to be taught to our children in their formative years, the truth be told about such doctrines, and that equal opportunity be given them to learn at the same time the eternal principles on which the American republic was found." The next day, Prentis traveled to Washington, D.C., for a meeting with his colleagues on the U.S. Chamber of Commerce

Subcommittee on Education, where he recited the same talking points that he had just given to the nation's oil tycoons. Clearly disturbed by Prentis's charges, the Committee members agonized about the danger of allowing educators "to dwell upon the weak spots" in the free enterprise system.*

In December 1940, NAM announced that it had hired Ralph W. Robey, Assistant Professor of Banking at Columbia University, to commission a textbook study to determine whether the nation's educational materials were providing students with an adequate understanding of "the private enterprise system" and its role in "the American way of life." His findings were outlined three months later, on February 22, 1941, in a *New York Times* front-page cover story. According to the article, "a substantial proportion" of American textbooks displayed "a lack of scholarly competence" and held "in derision or contempt" the system of free enterprise. Robey in particular was quoted as saying that "[t]he large proportion of the books seem to be written by persons who are not real authorities in their fields. What seems to me to be a substantial proportion place their emphasis upon our defects, on the short comings of our country, rather than on strong points of

* NAM's PR efforts weren't just limited to education. Kevin Krause's fantastic book, *One Nation Under God*, chronicles of the critical role that NAM played in using religion as a means of "regaining the upper hand in their war with Roosevelt." As Krause explains, the idea of America as a "nation under God" has its genesis in a NAM meeting that took place just a month after Pentis's meeting with the Chamber of Commerce.

the government and our business system."[184]

The Robey investigation precipitated an immediate and widespread reaction. John E. Wade, acting superintendent of schools in New York, ordered a "sweeping investigation" of all city-adopted social science textbooks that had been identified by Robey and his assistants. At a school in Englewood, New Jersey—where Forbes presided as a school board member—Rugg was called as a witness during a "schoolbook trial" to defend his educational philosophy. In San Diego, a state grand jury was convened to investigate charges of communism levied against Rugg and his teachings. The grand jury report, released in January 1941, "found that [Rugg's] books had a tendency to tear down the democratic form of government" and "recommend[ed] that the book be not used in public schools."[185] And on May 2, 1941, the American Legion adopted a recommendation of its Americanism Committee, publicly denouncing a number of social science textbooks, including Rugg's, as "not suitable for use in our schools since they oppose the American tradition."[186]

Under the glare of the communism and the insidious eye of corporate America, Rugg and his philosophy of social reconstruction quickly fell from grace. The American Legion boasted that by 1943, it had successfully ousted Rugg's textbooks from approximately 1,500 communities. And by mid-century, Rugg's textbook series had all but disappeared from

American schools entirely.[187*]

* * *

The story of Harold Rugg embodies, in a significant sense, the version of cultural decline described by Oswald Spengler in his famous work of 1918-1922, *The Decline of the West*. A culture is first born, Spengler tells us, when "a great soul awakens;" when a "central Idea" renders all things possible. "But," he says, "its living existence, that sequence of great epochs which define and display the stages of fulfilment, is an inner passionate struggle to maintain the Idea against the powers of Chaos without and the unconscious muttering deep-down within." Every culture in human history eventually reaches a twilight period where its central Idea "hardens" and "becomes Civilisation, the thing which we feel and understand in the words

---

* I must note here that I find Rugg's story to be extremely demoralizing, almost overwhelmingly so. In 1940, H. W. Prentis, Jr.—the NAM president who launched the anti-Rugg campaign—was named by then-Attorney General and eventual Supreme Court Justice Robert Jackson as "a leading native Fascist," an "underminer[] of morale," and an "economic exploiter[]" who attacked American democratic institutions throughout his tenure at NAM. According to Jackson, Prentis expressly stated that "hope for the future of our republic does not lie in more and more democracy." Congressman Adolph Sabath, then-Dean of the House of Representatives, likewise branded Prentis "a leading American Fascist." For a daunting look at NAM and the role it played in supporting the Third Reich, see *Facts and Fascism* (1941) by investigative journalist George Seldes.

Egypticism, Byzantinism, Mandarinism" and, one might add, Americanism. It is here that civilization finds it essential spirit; its particular way of life. But it is also stripped of its essence—the central Idea that awakened the culture in the first place.[188]

It is not unreasonable to suggest that the American twilight phase has its origins in the World War II era, when the Bernagie singularity merged with a vicious corporate assault on reason to build the groundwork for the malignant form of Americanism that we live with today. In fact, John Dewey—the forefather of twentieth century education in America—and influential columnist Walter Lippmann engaged in a heated public debate on this very topic in the 1920s. Lippmann felt that the extraordinary efficacy of propaganda demonstrated quite clearly that Americans were incapable of performing their responsibilities as citizens, at least insofar as the Founders had intended them to. For Lippmann, "the herd" was simply too ignorant to participate in democracy beyond selecting between "tweedledee and tweedledum."[189] Dewey sharply disagreed; he thought, as FDR later did, that man's irrationality could be mitigated by education. He believed that when "the individual joins with others in common effort, his intellectual and moral faculties are expanded," and thus he may become, through proper instruction, a meaningful participant in democracy.[190] The curriculum devised by Dr. Rugg reflected Dewey's hope for America. By teaching students about the dangers of propaganda and alerting them to the vainglory of corporate America, Rugg's curriculum was designed precisely to combat Lippmann's fears of an irrational populous.

The silencing of Rugg set America on a worrisome course. And yet, for a few brief moments in the twentieth century, there was hope that a new America would emerge; one fueled by equality and guided by reason. As the historian Arthur M. Schlesinger, Jr., wrote of the Kennedy years: "The capital city, somnolent in the Eisenhower years, had suddenly come alive" with "the release of energy which occurs when men with ideas have a chance to put them into practice."[191] "I look forward to a great America," Kennedy said in October 1963, "a future in which our country will match its military strength with our moral restraint, its wealth with our wisdom, its power with our purpose. I look forward to an America which will not be afraid of grace and beauty, . . . which will reward achievement in the arts as we reward achievement in business or statecraft."[192] According to Kennedy biographer Robert Dallek, JFK, like de Tocqueville, "knew that American self-interest and idealism were not mutually exclusive; indeed, one was as much part of the national tradition as the other."[193]

Over the course of his 1,000 days in office, Kennedy launched initiatives that brought Americans together in a unified quest for peace and progress. Addressing students at Rice University in 1962, Kennedy challenged those who questioned America's role in the race to space: "Why, some say the moon? Why choose this as our goal? And they may well ask, why climb the highest mountain? Why, thirty-five years ago, fly the Atlantic? . . . We choose to go to the moon in this decade, and do the other things, not because they are easy, but because they are hard; because that goal will serve to organize and measure the best of our energies and skills, because that challenge is one that we are willing to accept, one we are unwilling to postpone, and one which we intend to win. . . ."[194]

Just as Kennedy sent man to the moon in a quest for progress, so too did he send Americans abroad in a quest for peace. Founded in 1961, the Peace Corps provided an outlet to the "immense reservoir of men and women" who were "anxious to sacrifice their energies and time and toil to the cause of world peace and human progress." "Every young American who participates in the Peace Corps," Kennedy said, "will know that he or she is sharing in the great common task of bring to man that decent way of life which is the foundation of freedom and a condition of peace."[195] To this day, the Peace Corps remains of fixture of American values. Since its inception, more than 220,000 Americans have spread peace and prosperity to 141 countries across the world, thus proving, as Kennedy hoped it would, that "if you do good, you'll do well."[196]

In the words of historian Alan Brinkley, "Kennedy reminds us of a time when the nation's capacities looked limitless, when its future seemed unbounded, when Americans believed that they could solve hard problems and accomplish bold deeds."[197] By the middle of 1963, 59 percent of Americans surveyed claimed that they had voted for Kennedy in 1960, a 10 percent hike from the 49.7 percent of voters who had actually done so. Kennedy's New Frontier ignited a magnetic sense of civic optimism across the country, with Americans from all walks of life enthusiastically embracing their obligations of citizenship.

Then lighting struck. "It was all gone now," Schlesinger lamented shortly after Kennedy's assassination: "the life-affirming, life-enhancing zest, the brilliance, the wit, the cool commitment, the steady purpose."[198] The assassination of President Kennedy, wrote Ted Sorensen in 1963, "represented an incalculable loss for the future."

Five years later, it looked for a brief moment as if optimism had returned. In the words of Hunter S. Thompson, a "New Consciousness" permeated American society in the spring of 1968 due to the moral leadership of Robert Kennedy and Martin Luther King, Jr. There was, as Dr. King said at Riverside Church, "a fierce urgency of now." Many Americans agreed with Dr. King that "a radical revolution of values" was necessary to "begin the shift from a thing-oriented society to a person-oriented society."

These same Americans naturally gravitated toward Robert Kennedy as well, who called on all Americans "to confront the poverty of satisfaction, purpose, dignity that afflicts us all." "Too much and for too long," Kennedy stressed, "we seemed to have surrendered personal excellence and community values in the mere accumulation of material things." But Kennedy also believed that "we as a people, are strong enough, we are brave enough to be told the truth of where we stand." For Kennedy, "confronting the truth" was a necessary prerequisite to achieving progress: "I don't want to win support of voters by hiding the American condition in false hopes or illusions. I want us to find out the promise of the future, what we can accomplish here in the United States, what this country does stand for and what is expected of us in the years ahead." And if truth and common purpose could "win in November," then all Americans could "begin a new period of time for the United States of America," a period they could look back upon "and say as they said of Plato: 'Joy was in those days, but to live.'"

Kennedy and Dr. King spoke those words in the early spring of 1968. Over the course of the next three months, an entire "generation of hyper-political young Americans"—a group zealous for justice and motivated by the pursuit of happiness—plunged "into a terminal stupor." Martin Luther King was shot in April. Bobby Kennedy was shot in June. Nixon was nominated in July on the back of the Southern Strategy, and by August "The Movement" was finished.[199] Shock and tragedy had officially distorted the soul of America. As

President Jimmy Carter said in 1979: "We were sure that ours was a nation of the ballot, not the bullet, until the murders of John Kennedy and Robert Kennedy and Martin Luther King, Jr. We were taught that our armies were always invincible and our causes were always just, only to suffer the agony of Vietnam. We respected the Presidency as a place of honor until the shock of Watergate. . . . These wounds are still very deep. They have never been healed."[200] Indeed, they have festered.

* * *

The intense apathy that followed two decades of assassination, war, and corruption fashioned a void in American society that allowed the Bernagie thinker to reappear as the country's cultural and spiritual torchbearer. And this new way of thinking reached its apotheosis in the form of the "Great Communicator," Ronald Reagan—an actor who, in the span of 20 years, rose from a salesman at GE to the Governor of California to the President of the United States. And let me stipulate here that I am not talking about Reagan the man. I am talking about Reagan the candidate, the wily politician who merchandised himself onto the 1980 GOP ticket at the same age (69) as our current president.

For our purposes, Reagan's story begins in Hollywood, California, in 1937. Not long after arriving in Central LA, Reagan—after posing for a few cigarette ads, no doubt a Bernays-inspired idea—enlisted in the

Army National Guard, where he was commissioned a second lieutenant in the cavalry. After the attack on Pearl Harbor, Reagan, then 31, enlisted in the Army Air Forces (AAF), but his lifelong nearsightedness rendered him ineligible for front-line duty. Seeking recourse elsewhere, he decided to join a propaganda effort created by the AAF to rally American support for the war.

The head of the AAF at the time, General Henry (Hap) Arnold, appropriated the power of Hollywood movies by creating, in 1942, The First Motion Picture Unit, a squadron of film industry professionals that would go on to produce more than 400 propaganda and training films during its lifetime. At a meeting in the spring of that year, Arnold reached out to Jack Warner and the Warner Bros. studio, where Reagan was under contract.[201] With his acting and military background, Reagan welcomed the idea of joining the Unit.

Reagan thrived in his newfound role as Army thespian. Over the course of the next several years, Reagan narrated or acted in a number of propaganda films, including, for instance, *Tokyo Target* (1942), a puff piece that glorified the formidable B-29 aircraft bomber. Playing the role of narrator, Reagan predicted that the "Japs'" efforts to impede America's B-29 bombing campaigns would be "as hopeless as trying to stop the flow of water at Niagara Falls." Three years later, the B-29 bomber *Enola Gay* dropped the first atomic bomb over Hiroshima.

Like Bernays, Reagan saw first-hand the critical role that propaganda played during wartime. After his acting career fizzled out, Reagan found the perfect outlet for his propaganda skills at General Electric—then the corporate vanguard of advertising in America who had naturally hired Bernays in 1929 to run their PR stunts.[202*] Reagan's tutor at GE was a man by the name of Lemuel Boulware. At the time, Boulware was very much concerned with the rising power of trade unions and the Justice Department's renewed emphasis on prosecuting antitrust violations. "We businessmen are bold and imaginative before commercial competition," Boulware told a group of students at Harvard Business School in 1949. But "we are cowardly and silent in public when confronted with union and other economic

* In 1929, GE signed Bernays "for the spectacular challenge of his career"—the 50th anniversary of Edison's invention of the electric light bulb. To sell the event, Bernays organized a PR committee and appointed President Herbert Hoover as its chairman. The celebration, dubbed the Light's Golden Jubilee, was held in Detroit, where Henry Ford served as host. In attendance were the "who's who of the industrial age," including President and Mrs. Hoover, JP Morgan, John D. Rockefeller Jr., Madame Curie, Orville Wright, and William Randolph Hearst. The event was broadcast around the country by NBC's Graham McNamee, who exuberantly described the shenanigans as follows: "Mr. Edison, has the two wires in his hands. Now he's reaching up to the old lamp. Now he is making the connection. Light! Light's Golden Jubilee has come to its triumphant climax. And now the lights are springing up on all sides, the modern lights of 1929. Outside we hear the crowd cheering. And I hope that you and your family are entering into the spirit of this great moment in history, the way we are. You can turn on your electric lights and add your personal tribute to that great outpouring of gratitude and personal affections which has made Light's Golden Jubilee the greatest tribute ever paid to any living man." And with that, Bernays got the whole world to turn on its lights at the same time.

and political doctrines contrary to our beliefs."[203] Boulware was right to be concerned. At the time, GE was facing no fewer than 13 antitrust prosecutions in the United States for price fixing and other corporate crimes.[204]

In order to combat the influence of organized labor, Boulware concocted a Bernaysian communications strategy that bypassed all interaction with union leadership in favor of speaking directly to GE workers about the virtues of anticommunism and free-market capitalism. The goal, as Boulware stated himself, was to turn the tens of thousands of employees at GE into "mass communicators" who would sell their friends and families on the notion that "what was good for GE was good for America," the hope being that they would thereafter elect public officials who would do the same.[205]

GE had learned from Bernays that "[t]he propagandist must treat personality as he would treat any other objective fact within his province." Thus, to full its propaganda mission, GE, in 1954, hired Reagan—then a New Deal Democrat who had recently starred opposite a chimpanzee in Hollywood's *Bedtime for Bonzo*—to be the face of the company, a role that Reagan later described as his "apprenticeship for public life."[206]

Reagan played two overlapping roles at GE, the most publicized of which was as host of *General Electric Theater*, a thirty-minute anthology series broadcast weekly on CBS that often involved Reagan nattering with Hollywood figures like Jimmy Stewart, Jack Benny, and Judy Garland. The program was an instant success, and by 1956–1957, it was one of the best-rated shows on TV, behind only *The Ed Sullivan Show* and *I Love Lucy*. The content, of course, was controlled by GE and choreographed to fit its commercial slogan: "Progress is our most important product."[207]

The second character that Reagan played at GE was that of "corporate ambassador." It was in this capacity that Reagan earned, in his own words, his "post-graduate education in political science." Over the course of his eight-year tenure, Reagan traveled to every one of GE's 135 plants to lecture Boulware's nationwide army of 250,000 communicators on the principles of GE's corporate ideology.[208] Combining homespun tales and timeworn anecdotes—some true, others not so much—with Boulware's brand of conservatism, Reagan sold his audiences on the dream of a bright future; one powered by GE.[209] As Reagan biographer Lou Cannon explains, "the script that emerged from this corporate-sponsored odyssey was patriotic, antigovernment, anticommunist, and probusiness, and was harmonized enough that it could be used before any audience anywhere in the country."* From this experience, Reagan—like Bernays—learned that it was far more powerful to appeal to an audience's

* As my friend Tom Brown points out, how can one be both antigovernment *and* patriotic?

emotions than it was to engage in rational debates about policy. And like Carnegie, Reagan came to understand that by smiling at his audience and speaking to them about "symbolic issues like freedom, personal autonomy, and traditional values," it was far easier to persuade the masses via influence than it was to do so via proof.[210]

By the time Reagan left GE in 1962, he had completed his transformation from FDR Democrat to GE conservative. But more importantly, he had sharpened his dog-whistle persuasion tactics that would carry him into the White House. Running for Governor of California in 1964, Reagan made one of the central themes of his campaign "the mess at Berkeley," a college where they held "sexual orgies so vile I cannot describe them to you." If elected, Reagan promised to "investigate the charges of communism and blatant sexual misbehavior on the Berkeley campus." Channeling his inner Bernays, Reagan discerned that "hidden away in the hearts of parents was the fear that their own children might one day go away to college, grow beards and march against authority."[211]

When discussing race, Reagan rarely used the term "black" or "African-American;" instead he peddled stereotypes—the "welfare queen," the "over sexualized woman," the "strapping young buck"—to draw Bernaysian connections between race and criminality. One of Reagan's aides, a scurvy consultant named Lee Atwater who would go on to be deputy campaign manager of the Reagan-Bush '84 Committee, gave an anonymous interview in 1981 in which he described Reagan's studied approach to racism. Drawing a comparison between The Gipper and Richard Nixon, Atwater explained: "You start out in 1954 by saying, 'Nigger, nigger, nigger.' By 1968 you can't say 'nigger'—that hurts you, backfires. So you say stuff like, uh, 'forced busing,' 'states' rights,' and all that stuff, and you're getting so abstract. Now, you're talking about cutting taxes, and all these things you're talking about are totally economic things and a byproduct of them is, blacks get hurt worse than whites. . . .'We want to cut this,' is much more abstract than even the busing thing, uh, and a hell of a lot more abstract than 'Nigger, nigger.'"[212]

Reagan's espousal of dog-whistle racism continues to be felt today. In associating poverty with race, President Reagan was able to reconceptualize the public debate surrounding the merits of welfare reform. In years past, welfare was viewed through the lens of assurance—it *provided* minimum income to those who needed it most. President Nixon, in 1969, proposed a guaranteed minimum income bill. His idea was later embraced by President Carter, who used Nixon's model in crafting his Program for Better Jobs and Income. Speaking to Congress in 1977, President Carter called on his legislative colleagues "to abolish our existing welfare system, and replace it with a job-oriented program for those able to work and a simplified, uniform, equitable cash assistance program for those in need who are unable to work by virtue of disability, age or family circumstance."[213] Under Reagan, however, the definition of welfare reform "changed from assuring a minimum income based only on need to getting people *off* welfare" (emphasis mine).[214] By the mid-1990s, "welfare" had become a code word for race, just like "crime."

Inspired by the hollow leadership of Newt Gingrich, Republican members of Congress launched an all-out assault on welfare during President Bill Clinton's first term. Representative John Mica (R-Florida), speaking on the House floor in 1995, analogized welfare recipients to "alligators." His colleague, Representative Barbara Cubin (R-Wyoming), offered a similarly vile analogy to describe what she called "the wolf welfare program." The federal government, Cubin cackled, "opened the gate to let the wolves out and now the wolves will not go. They are cutting the fence down to make the wolves go out and the wolves will not go."[215]

In 1996—after vetoing two previous welfare reform bills—President Clinton fulfilled his campaign promise to "end welfare as we know it" by signing into law the Personal Responsibility and Work Opportunity Reconciliation Act. Clinton's welfare bill repealed the longstanding Aid to Families with Dependent Children program that had been passed under the 1935 Social Security Act and replaced it with the Temporary Assistance to Needy Families program. The new bill imposed time limits on welfare assistance, barred thousands of immigrants from receiving disability and old-age assistance and food stamps, and reduced food-stamp assistance for millions of children in working families. Senator Ted Kennedy described the bill as "legislative child abuse." The nonpartisan Center on Budget and Policy Priorities agreed, calling it "probably the single harshest provision written into a major safety net program in at least 30 years." Peter Edelman, who Clinton appointed as assistant secretary for planning and evaluation at the Department of Health and Human Services, resigned in protest. Clinton's bill, Edelman said shortly after its passing, gave "new meaning to the word 'draconian'" and was "*the* major milestone in the political race to the bottom."[216]

Clinton's genuflection to the obduracy caucus set a precedent for governance that has only grown more perverse in the two decades since his presidency. In 2010, Senator Addison M. McConnell gave an interview with the *National Journal* in which he proclaimed that "the single most important thing we want to achieve is for President Obama to be a one-term president." Asked whether that meant "endless, or less frequent, confrontation" with Obama, McConnell responded that it would not be "inappropriate for us to do business with him" so long as "President Obama does a Clintonian backflip."[217]

Reagan's legacy continues to be felt in other ways. Throughout his political career, he intuitively triggered voters' deepest fears by drawing false parallels between policies with which he disagreed and policies implemented by tyrants—the same approach that prompted Benjamin Franklin to issue his celebrated call for civility during the Constitutional Convention two centuries prior. In 1976, Reagan audaciously proclaimed that "Fascism was really the basis of the New Deal," an allegation that he then repeated several times as president. During an interview with Ben Wattenberg of PBS in 1981, for example, Reagan doubled down on this accusation, declaring "that President Roosevelt's advisers admired the fascist system. . . . They thought that private ownership with government management and control á la the Italian system was the way to go, and that has been evident in all their writings." As the *Washington Post* reported at the time, Reagan did not "cite a reference" to support his claim that FDR's advisors admired fascism and "research efforts . . . failed to find any."[218]* "As the hard days come upon him," the *Post* remarked, Reagan "is reverting to type, quick to utter the brutal, damaging word. He has not learned to bite his tongue. He smiles when he says these things. Apparently, it makes all the difference."[219]

Reagan's false equivalency in this regard is particularly alarming. As George Orwell wrote in *Politics and the English Language*, if "you don't know what Fascism is, how can you struggle against

* The irony, of course, is that many *opponents* of the New Deal provided direct assistance to the Third Reich, *e.g.*, Fred Koch.

Fascism?"[220] The New Deal was to Fascism what the Emancipation Proclamation was to slavery. Hitler responded to economic depression with the Reichstag fire; President Roosevelt responded with the New Deal—Hitler put human beings in an oven; FDR put human beings to work.

Like Carnegie's pupils, Reagan was full of "personality" and devoid of substance. As Elizabeth Drew of *The New Yorker* observed in 1976, his appeal "has to do not with competence at governing but with the emotion he evokes." Reagan concurred. "I'm not an intellectual," he professed during a 1985 interview with the *New York Times*. President Nixon, for whom Reagan had given more than 200 speeches during the 1960 presidential campaign,[221] was particularly apprehensive about Reagan's empty suit persona—a concern he expressed during an unguarded conversation with National Security Advisor Henry Kissinger in 1971:

> President Nixon: What's your evaluation of Reagan after meeting him several times now?
>
> Kissinger: Well, I think he's a—actually I think he's a pretty decent guy.
>
> President Nixon: Oh, decent, no question, but his brains. . . .

Kissinger: Well, his brains, are negligible. I—

President Nixon: He's really pretty shallow, Henry.

Kissinger: He's shallow. He's got no . . . he's an actor. He—When he gets a line he does it very well. He said, "Hell, people are remembered not for what they do, but for what they say. Can't you find a few good lines?" [Chuckles.] That's really an actor's approach to foreign policy–to substantive. . . .

President Nixon: I've said a lot of good things, too, you know damn well.

Kissinger: Well, that too.

. . .

President Nixon: It shows you how a man of limited mental capacity simply doesn't know what the Christ is going on in the foreign area.[222]

The consummate salesmen, Reagan cynically believed that he was better off "practicing one-liners" because "viewers would be more apt to remember a deft phrase than a technical argument."[223] As such, the acquisition of genuine knowledge was purposefully avoided. Whereas Abraham Lincoln—in the words of his biographer William Herndon—"ate up, digested, and assimilated" Francis Wayland's *Elements of Political Economy* in an effort to gain a deeper understanding of economic theory,[224] Reagan developed his economic views in Hollywood: "I think my own experience with our tax laws in Hollywood probably taught me more about practical economic theory than I ever learned in a classroom or from an economist," he earnestly avowed in his 1990 biography, *American Life*.[225] In 1981, shortly after his administration presented Congress with his "voodoo economics" proposal (George H.W. Bush's term)—one that added $120 billion to the federal deficit in just three years by simultaneously slashing capital gains and estate taxes for the wealthy and increasing payroll taxes for the middle class—his treasury secretary "acknowledged that the highly optimistic forecast was based on Administration economists' views of how Americans are likely to respond to the program and *not on any existing model*" (emphasis mine).[226] In an apt Freudian slip, Reagan confessed his reality-distorting approach to governance when he misquoted John Adams during the Republican National Convention in 1988: "Facts are stupid things—stubborn things, I should say."[227]

The most durable impact that Reagan had on

politics, however, was his approach to advertising. In 1983, he combined his seat-of-your-pants governing strategy with a cutting-edge campaign apparatus that fully embraced the Bernagie singularity. As he prepared to launch his reelection campaign, his Gallup Poll approval rating stood at 35 percent, equal to President Lyndon Johnson's at its nadir during the Vietnam War. The federal deficit had more than doubled during Reagan's first term, opening him up to criticism for failing to keep his promise to restore the American economy. Voter support for Republicans was waning as well. Using the slogan "Stay the course," the Grand Old Party lost 26 House seats and seven governorships in the 1982 midterm elections. Reagan realized that in order to get reelected, he had to sell the country on the notion that, under his leadership, good times were returning to the United States.

In 1984, his campaign aired a one-minute commercial called "Morning in America" that presidential historian Michael Beschloss recently characterized as "one of the most effective campaign spots ever broadcast." As Beschloss perceptively described the ad: "The scenes in 'Morning' would have fit almost seamlessly into the 1950s sitcoms 'Father Knows Best' or 'Leave It to Beaver. . . .' Set to the music of sentimental strings, the ad images include a paperboy on his bicycle, a family taking a rolled rug into a house and campers raising an American flag. The subtext is that after 20 years of social tumult, assassinations, riots, scandal, an unpopular war and gas lines, Mr. Reagan returned the United States to the tranquillity of the 1950s." At the start of the ad, the narrator's euphonious voice says: "It's morning again in America. Today more men and women will go to work than ever before in our country's history." Such wording was, of course, categorically misleading. As Beschloss notes, the ad's suggestion that "more men and women" were going to work actually "reflected the growth *of the American population* in four years" (emphasis mine). From an economic standpoint, unemployment remained higher (at about 7.5 percent) than it was Jimmy Carter left office.

Unlike earlier presidential campaigns—which outsourced messaging strategies to existing advertising agencies—Reagan's was the first to construct its own internal advertising organization. Undoubtedly recalling the success of The First Motion Picture Unit during World War II and Boulware's "mass communicators" initiative during the Red Scare, Reagan's campaign hired Phil Dusenberry—the executive director of the ad agency, BBDO, who had been a screenwriter for "The Natural" and was responsible for popular slogans like GE's "We Bring Good Things to Life" and Pepsi's "The Choice of a New Generation"—to lead 40 advertising "stars" in crafting Reagan's reelection image. Sitting at Rockefeller Center, the cadre of advertising gurus crafted the Morning in America ad by implementing the exact same tactics that

Reagan had used at GE. The narrator proudly "boasted that interest rates were about half those of 1980, and that about 2,000 families a day were buying homes." Then, over prepossessing wedding images, the narrator said, "This afternoon, 6,500 young men and women will be married," as if the number of marriages per day was indicative of economic prosperity. "Under the leadership of President Reagan," the ad concluded, "our country is prouder, and stronger, and better. Why would we ever want to return to where we were less than four short years ago?" Reagan himself is merely afterthought in the ad; his face appears for two or three seconds at the end—a still color photo on a campaign button, next to an American flag. Nevertheless, the commercial was immensely influential, a fact that befuddled Walter Mondale on the campaign trail: "It's all picket fences and puppy dogs. No one's hurting. No one's alone. No one's hungry. No one's unemployed. No one gets old. Everybody's happy."

As Beschloss observes, Reagan's 1984 campaign, 30-plus years later, is still "largely remembered for that one commercial. . . . [I]t captivated many voters and helped push many of Mr. Reagan's problems to the periphery. In today's fractured media universe, it is unlikely that a single paid TV spot will again approach that kind of *influence*" (emphasis mine).[228]

Whether another commercial will top Reagan's Morning in America ad remains to be seen, but what cannot be denied is the monumental role that corporate

America plays in shaping our country's social and political perceptions. The budget of Reagan's 1984 reelection committee totaled $20.2 million. According to the head of the committee, John Buckley, that money was distributed evenly across five focus areas—"voter registration, advertising, establishing 50 state headquarters, travel, and national headquarters expenses."[229] Conspicuously absent from this list is anything remotely related to *policy*. Reagan's campaign, by design, flouted the most important consideration in democracy—the common good.

Having spent eight years under Reagan's tutelage, George H. W. Bush assumed the presidency well-versed in Bernays's propaganda principles. In the fall of 1990, as Saddam Hussein's occupation of Kuwait reached its six-month anniversary, President Bush found himself having a difficult time garnering public support for the deployment of American troops to the Middle East. That changed, however, on October 10, 1990, when a 15-year-old girl from Kuwait gave a tearful, moving testimony before the Congressional House Human Rights Caucus. The girl, Nayirah (she would only give her first name), said that she had been a volunteer at a hospital in Kuwait City, where she had seen Iraqi troops rip scores of babies out of incubators, leaving them "to die on the cold floor." Fighting back tears, Nayirah described the incident as "horrifying." Representative John Porter (R-Illinois), who chaired the committee, said after Nayirah's testimony, "We have never heard, in all this time, in all circumstances, a record of inhumanity, and brutality, and sadism, as the ones that [Nayirah has] given us today."

45 million Americans watched Nayirah's shocking testimony that evening on ABC's "Nightline" and NBC's "Nightly News." In the days and weeks that followed, seven senators cited her story in arguing for U.S. military involvement in Kuwait (leading to a congressional resolution that passed by *five* votes), and President Bush repeated the story on 10 separate occasions. When the Gulf War began in January 1991, 92 percent of Americans supported Bush's decision.

Years later, it emerged that the incubator story was a big, boldfaced, Bernaysian lie. The refugee was no refugee. She was Nayirah al-Sabah, the daughter of the Kuwaiti ambassador to the United States. Her testimony was arranged by a group called Citizens for a Free Kuwait, a front for the Kuwaiti government. With the help of John Porter and Representative Tom Lantos (D-California), Citizens hired Hill & Knowlton—a New York-based PR firm well known for its work on behalf of the tobacco industry—to "devise a campaign to win American support for the war." Subsequent research by the firm, which cost $1 million, indicated that Americans would be particularly responsive to stories about "atrocities" committed against babies.* So the incubator tale was concocted, the witness was coached,

* Real shocker there.

and off America went to war.[230] "It was a bright cold day in April," begins *1984,* "and the clocks were striking thirteen."

The entire scheme tied back to both Reagan and Bernays. Craig Fuller, the president and COO of Hill & Knowlton, was George H.W. Bush's vice presidential chief of staff during Reagan's presidency. And John Hill, the co-founder of the firm, succeeded Bernays as the PR chief for the American tobacco industry during the 1950s. To this day, Hill & Knowlton continues to manufacture consent by adhering to the Bernaysian propaganda doctrine. "PR practitioners today have a host of new tools that they can use to socialize consent," the firm posted on its website in 2013, "but understanding the historical context of our profession helps us better grasp the philosophical and ethical underpinnings of our industry. Much of what Bernays had to say more than sixty years ago still has relevance today when designing a PR strategy and campaign."[231]

Rather than stopping the Bernagie thinker in its tracks, Bill Clinton replaced Reagan and Bush as its standard-bearer in the 1990s. According to George Stephanopoulos, the political and moral backflip that Clinton performed during the welfare crisis was largely the product of his decision to hire Republican strategist Dick Morris as an advisor after the 1994 mid-terms. "Over the course of the first nine months of 1995," said Stephanopoulos, "no single person had more power over the president, and therefore over the government, than Dick Morris—no question about it."

Morris, a cousin of Roy Cohn, began advising Clinton in 1994 by calling into the Oval Office under the code name "Charlie." His advice was straight out of the Carnegie playbook. "Dick Morris was telling [Clinton] to buck up his confidence," Stephanopoulos said. "Perfect example of the stage direction coming out of the actor's mouth, as opposed to the script." In 1995—after Clinton met with self-help guru Tony Robbins (or "Robinson," as Stephanopoulos calls him)—Morris persuaded Clinton to adopt a "triangulation" approach to governance, which Stephanopoulos described as treating "Democrats and Republicans in the House alike, as if they were both adversaries," so that Clinton could "push off either one in equal measure and appear to be above the political fray." This methodology was, in Stephanopoulos's words, "empty of substance" and "amoral." But Morris deemed it necessary for Clinton's political survival. When the Republicans' welfare bill reached Clinton's desk in 1996—a moment that Stephanopoulos described as a "kind of 'Custer's last stand' for liberal Democrats"—it was Dick Morris who had the President's ear: "Everyone knew that Dick Morris was sitting up there in the White House saying, 'If you [don't] sign this, Mr. President, you will lose.'" Clinton, of course, heeded Morris's advice.[232]

Clinton, clearly valuing Morris's jejune political opinions, decided to appoint Morris as head of his 1996 reelection campaign. The parallels between Clinton and

Reagan's reelection efforts are striking. As Morris conceitedly explains in his book *Behind the Oval Office*, the "key to Clinton's victory" wasn't the President's legislative track record or the economy; it was Clinton's "early television advertising. There has never been anything even remotely like it in the history of Presidential elections." With a then-staggering $85 million adverting budget,* Morris exults, "We created the first fully advertised Presidency in U.S. history."[233]

The entire apparatus was pure Bernays. Morris was convinced that the only way to capture the swing vote was "to forget all ideology and instead turn politics into a form of consumer business." As he told Clinton, "Politics needs to be as responsive to the whims and the desires of the marketplace [just as] business is. And it needs to be sensitive to the bottom line—profits or votes—as a business is."

Employing what he called a "consumer rules philosophy," Morris told Clinton that he needed to "make a symbolic sacrifice of the old politics to convince the swing voters to trust him." Clinton agreed. As Election Day approached, Clinton, among other things, ordered his Secretary of Education to promote "religious observance" on public-school grounds and signed into law the Defense of Marriage Act, a conservative bill that permitted states to outlaw same-sex marriages. These accomplishments were then

* The presidential candidates in 2016 spent a combined $4.4 *billion* on TV ads.

"formulated" into a nationwide propaganda narrative that billed Clinton as "values" president.

This Bernaysian approach, in the words of Robert Reich, regarded voters merely as a "collection of individual desires that had to be catered to and pandered to." For Morris and Clinton, Reich explained, Americans were nothing more than "irrational . . . bundles of unconscious emotion" that could persuaded only by appealing to their anxieties and desires.

The effectiveness of this approach, however, was extraordinary. With Morris at the helm, Clinton's ratings among swing voters soared. Morris continued to craft Clinton's image over the next several months, writing speeches and boosting Clinton's confidence, until he was forced to step down in August 1996 after reports surfaced that he had allowed a prostitute to listen in on his conversations with the President. Nevertheless, the Clinton/Gore ticket secured the nomination over Bob Dole and Jack Kemp, giving Clinton another four years in the White House.[234]

* * *

Meanwhile, an arrant populous propelled by fantasy, mysticism, individuality, identity, mutiny, and obscurity—all tenets that were beyond the pale for the Founders—continued to propagate across the country. Its characteristics are unadorned. It reveals itself through moral overstrain, resentment, self-assurance, and a curious, almost maniacal, lack of humor. It is the most direct consequence of Reagan's propaganda machine; one rooted in illusory "values" and superficial "patriotism" and devoid of reason or curiosity. Clinton, in chimerical fashion, adopted this anti-intellectual strategy throughout the 1990s before passing the buck to George W. Bush, who slipped through the Supreme Court and into the White House using the same approach. "See," he said shortly after securing a second term, "in my line of work you got to keep repeating things over and over and over again for the truth to sink in, to kind of catapult the propaganda."[235]

Bush's cavalier use of "truth" in the same sentence as "propaganda" is deeply unsettling. Propaganda, as we know from Bernays, is untruth; it is designed to manipulate. The fact that the President of the United States sought election to the highest office in the land by "catapulting the propaganda" is nothing short of Orwellian, and its effects bear a chilling resemblance to what Hannah Arendt described in *The Origins of Totalitarianism* shortly after the fall of the Third Reich:

> In an ever-changing, incomprehensible world the masses had reached the point where they would, at the same time, believe everything and nothing, think that everything was possible and that nothing was true. . . . Mass propaganda discovered that its audience was ready at

> all times to believe the worst, no matter how absurd, and did not particularly object to being deceived because it held every statement to be a lie anyhow. The totalitarian mass leaders based their propaganda on the correct psychological assumption that, under such conditions, one could make people believe the most fantastic statements one day, and trust that if the next day they were given irrefutable proof of their falsehood, they would take refuge in cynicism; instead of deserting the leaders who had lied to them, they would protest that they had known all along that the statement was a lie and would admire the leaders for their superior tactical cleverness.

By catapulting the propaganda, George Bush helped to create a new category of American voters. For the better part of the past two centuries, debates about democratic competence focused on two types of voters—informed (knowledgeable) and uninformed (ignorant). Today, however, tens of millions of Americans are demonstrably *mis*informed. According to researchers at Dartmouth College, a misinformed voter is someone who holds "factual beliefs that are false or contradict the best available evidence in the public domain." In contrast to uninformed voters, individuals who are misinformed hold their misperceptions "with a high degree of certainty and consider themselves to be well-informed about the fact in question."[236] Or, as my dad puts it, "always wrong, never in doubt."

As an example of a common "misperception," the Dartmouth scholars point to a study examining individuals' responses to the U.S. military's failure to discover weapons of mass destruction (WMD) after Operation Iraqi Freedom in 2003. "While most respondents believe correctly that WMD were not found," the authors write, "Democrats and Republicans interpreted this fact differently: Democrats inferred that Saddam Hussein did not possess WMD immediately before the invasion, while Republicans inferred that the weapons had been moved, destroyed, or had not yet been discovered. The latter interpretation is inconsistent with the best available evidence and we therefore define it as a misperception."[237]

Americans' misperceptions are not limited to the Iraq War. Recent studies show that one in five Americans "confidently holds misperceptions" about the largest holder of the U.S. debt, changes in debt and deficits, the federal tax burden, and time limits on welfare benefits. Likewise, many citizens falsely believe that universal background checks are currently mandated under existing law, while a substantial number of Americans reject widespread evidence that earth's climate is warming.[238] This crisis of objectivity has created what many have dubbed a "post-truth" society; one where facts are inherently relative and judgments are guided by emotion rather than reason.

One of the most troubling aspects of this irrational confidence disease is that it tends to exacerbate in the face of contradictory evidence—a phenomenon often referred to as the "backfire effect." This concept has its origins in a 1957 work written by three social psychologists, Leon Festinger, Henry Riecken, and Stanley Schacter, called *Why Prophecy Fails*. Chapter 1 begins as follows: "A man with a conviction is a hard man to change. Tell him you disagree and he turns away. Show him facts or figures and he questions your sources. Appeal to logic and he fails to see your point. . . . Suppose that he is presented with evidence, unequivocal and undeniable evidence, that his belief is wrong: what will happen? The individual will frequently emerge, not only unshaken, but even more convinced of the truth of his beliefs than ever before."[239]

Again the Iraq War offers a useful example. In one study, respondents were given a mock news article in which President Bush defended the Iraq War by warning (as he in fact did) that there "was a risk, a real risk, that Saddam Hussein would pass weapons of materials or information to terrorist networks." After reading the article, the participants were asked to peruse the Pentagon's Duelfer Report, which documented the lack of WMD in Iraq. Once they were finished reading the report, the participants were instructed to state their agreement on a five-point scale (from "strongly agree" to "strongly disagree") with the following statement: Iraq "had an active weapons of mass destruction program, the ability to produce these weapons, and large stockpiles of WMD." For liberal subjects, there was a modest shift toward disagreement with this statement, mainly because they already tended to disagree with it. But for those who characterized themselves as conservative, there was a statistically significant shift in the direction of *agreeing* with the statement. "In other words," the researchers concluded, "the correction backfired—conservatives who received a correction telling them that Iraq did not have WMD were more likely to believe that Iraq *had* WMD than those in the control condition" (emphasis mine).[240]

Liberals are by no means immune from the backfire effect. In 2005, many liberals incorrectly believed that President Bush had imposed a ban on stem cell research. When presented with correction evidence from the *New York Times* or foxnews.com, they doubled down on their views. Conservatives, by contrast, accepted the correction.[241] "One believes things," wrote Huxley, "because one has been conditioned to believe them."[242]

The neurological implications of this informational contingency are similarly troublesome. In December 2016, three neuroscientists—Jonas Kaplan, Sarah Gimbel and Sam Harris—published a paper entitled *Neural Correlates of Maintaining One's Political Beliefs in the Face of Counterevidence* that shows, with MRI imaging, what happens on a neurological level when one's political beliefs are challenged. According to the study—which was conducted on 40 self-declared liberals—"[w]hen people's political beliefs are challenged, their brains become active in areas that govern personal identity and emotional responses to threats." As a result, "beliefs that relate to one's social identity are likely to be more difficult to change."[243] As lead author Jonas Kaplan explains, "Political beliefs are like religious beliefs in the respect that both are part of who you are and important for the social circle to which you belong. To consider an alternative view, you would have to consider an alternative version of yourself."[244] Dale Kahan, professor of psychology and law at Yale, offers a similar analogy: "Most people have no reason to have a position on climate change aside from expression of their identity. Their personal behavior isn't going to affect the risk that they face. They don't matter enough as a voter to determine the outcome on policies or anything like this. These are just badges of membership in these groups, and that's how most people process the information."[245] Bernays, of course, discerned this phenomenon four score ago: "The average citizen is the world's most efficient censor," he wrote in *Crystallizing Public Opinion*. "His own mind is the greatest barrier between him and the facts. His own 'logic-proof compartments,' his own absolutism are the obstacles which prevent him from seeing in terms of experience and thought rather than in terms of group reaction."[246]

Facts, in other words, assume a sort of duality in the public sphere. Harvard Professor Cass Sustein calls this illogical dyad an "informational cascade." "In an informational cascade," he writes, "people cease relying at a certain point on their private information or opinions. They decide instead on the basis of the signals conveyed by others. It follows that the behavior of the first few people, or even one, can in theory produce similar behavior from countless followers." And because we tend to identify as members of a political "team," facts that call into question our loyalty to that team necessarily force us to choose between acquiring knowledge on one hand and safeguarding identity on the other. As the psychologist Thomas Gilovich writes, "When examining evidence relevant to a given belief, people are inclined to see what they expect to see, and conclude what they expect to conclude. . . . For desired conclusions, we ask ourselves, '*Can* I believe this?,' but for unpalatable conclusions we ask, '*Must* I believe this?'"[247]

This strikingly irrational dilemma runs the other way too. If we find ourselves surrounded by a group of friends who hold misperceptions about a particular fact, and we know what the truth is, we nonetheless "go along with the crowd in order to maintain the good opinion of others."[248] In other words, we pull a Carnegie: "The only way to get the best of an argument is to avoid it."

* * *

Our current state of mass unreason contains a cruel paradox: those who have succumbed to the Bernagie-style leadership approach—a group that is no doubt bipartisan—are the ones who have suffered the most over the past 40 years. Reagan's neoliberal platform of small government, tax cuts, deregulation, free trade, and monetarist financial policies—which was subsequently embraced by Bush Sr., Clinton, and Bush Jr.—broke the back of FDR's New Deal and with it government's commitment to protect the poor and middle class against economic hardship. "The fact is that income inequality is real," George Bush finally confessed in 2007. "It's been rising for more than 25 years." This democratization of inequality created what Nobel Prize-winning economist Paul Krugman memorably dubbed "the Great Divergence." "The divergent fortunes of the rich and the middle class became such a fact of everyday life that people seldom noticed it," writes Timothy Noah in his Krugman-inspired book of the same title, "except perhaps to observe now and then with a shrug that life was unfair."[249]

Recall that for a large chunk of American history, the notion of economic prosperity was tied to the concept of production. Increases in the latter meant more of the former. But today that is no longer the case. "Since 1978," Princeton's Alan Blinder wrote in 2010, "productivity in the nonfarm business sector is up 86 percent, but real compensation per hour (which includes fringe benefits) is up just 37 percent. Does that seem fair?" Of course not. A minute percentage of the population has become radically wealthy on the backs of the poor and middle class. And as Timothy Noah writes, "When ordinary people have nothing to gain from the fruits of their labor even in times of economic growth, the only motivation they have to perform their jobs well is fear of destitution."[250]

The economists Thomas Piketty, Emmanuel Saez and Gabriel Zucman recently put a face on this radical inequality with their "hockey-stick graph" (reproduced with the authors' permission on the next page). It shows that the poor and middle class, prior to 1980, saw their income increase on an annual basis by a post-inflation, after-taxes rate of roughly 2 percent a year. At that rate, a household's income nearly doubles every 34 years. The rich, meanwhile, saw their income increase at an annual rate below 1 percent, meaning that their take-home pay was rising more slowly than the rest of the country. Taken together, the average income growth across the country was roughly 2.0 percent.

Since 1980, however, the national average for income growth has remained about the same (1.4 percent), but the growth for the wealthiest Americans (the top 1/40th of the income distribution) has more than quintupled, while everyone else's has dropped.[251]

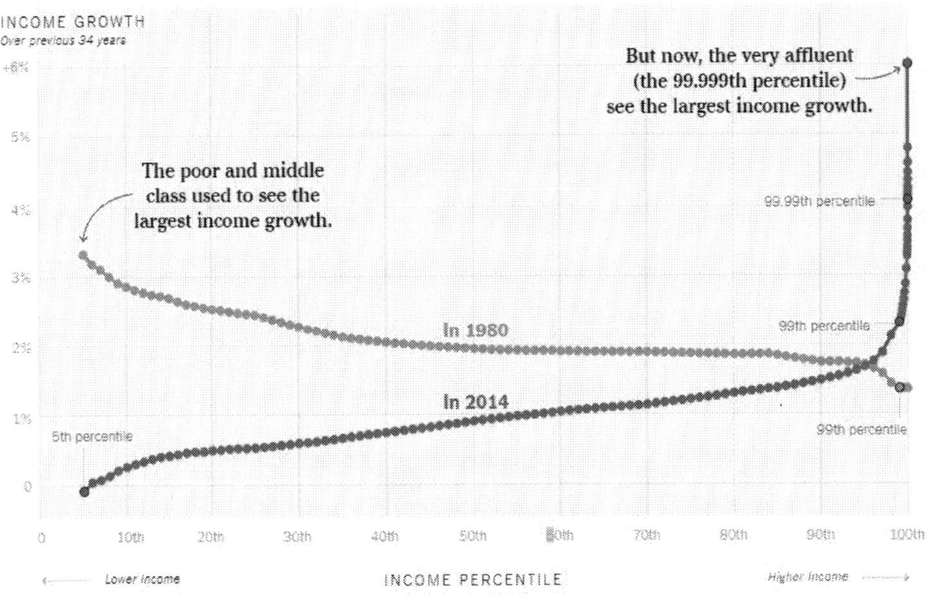

Note: Inflation-adjusted annual average growth using income after taxes, transfers and non-cash benefits.

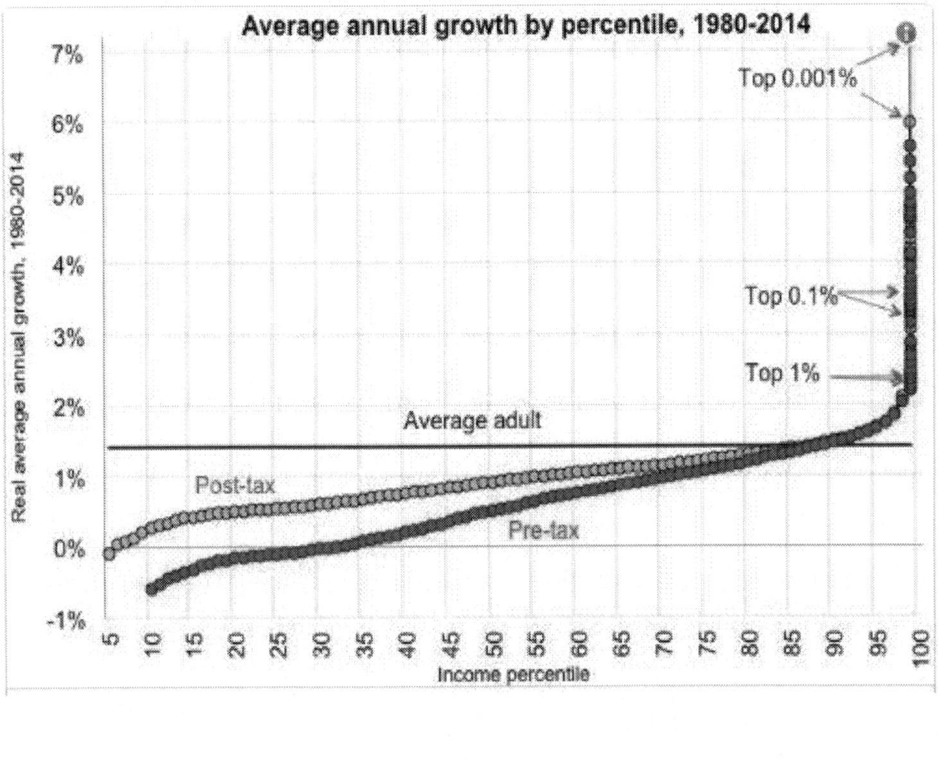

Average annual growth by percentile, 1980-2014

Real average annual growth, 1980-2014

7%
6%
5%
4%
3%
2%
1%
0%
-1%

Top 0.001%
Top 0.1%
Top 1%
Average adult
Post-tax
Pre-tax

5 10 15 20 25 30 35 40 45 50 55 60 65 70 75 80 85 90 95 100

Income percentile

This is the power of propaganda. It forces us to violate the truth. It tranquillizes reason into a state of inertia and makes people believe that they are acting in their own best interests when they are objectively acting *against* their own best interests. It masks truth because of the danger truth represents—*obsequium amicos, veritas odium parit;* obsequiousness makes friends, the truth creates enemies. And what makes this particular form of unreason so unsettling—as journalist Sam Adler-Bell acutely observes—is that "acting with your gut is a rational political choice if you're hungry."[252]

With millions of people acting with their gut, America has propelled itself into a social and economic spiral. Since 2016, life expectancy has declined, suicide rates have risen, the opioid crisis has worsened, inequality has grown, and confidence in government has fallen. 63 percent of Americans don't have enough money in savings to cover a $500 health care expense. 28 percent of working-age adults have no retirement savings whatsoever. 32 percent of Millenials still live at home, which is not surprising given that they have taken on 300 percent more student-loan debt than their parents.[253]

The moral fabric of our country is unraveling. Economist Jeffrey Sachs, director of the UN Sustainable Development Solutions Network, sees a crisis brewing. "I think there really is a deep and very unsettling signal coming through that U.S. society is in many ways under profound stress, even though the economy by traditional measures is doing fine," he said in March 2018. "The trends are not good, and the comparative position of the U.S. relative to other high-income countries is nothing short of alarming." Meanwhile, those living in the Nordic nations are happier than anyone in the world. Why? According to Dr. Sachs, they have "solid social support systems [and] good public services," both of which are funded by citizens paying "a significant amount in taxes."[254]

Without hope or economic stability, how can we expect misinformed citizens to commit themselves to the toil of reason? Democratic education, as we know from Montesquieu, is onerous; one cannot find the common good without knowing how, where, or, most importantly, *why*, to look for it.

* * *

"Power," as Orwell tells us, "is in tearing human minds to pieces and putting them together again in new shapes of your own choosing." During the 1980s, the country's leading propaganda experts sold voters on Reagan the same way Bernays sold consumers on Lucky Strikes. And Reagan himself sold his regressive economic plan to voters the same way a Carnegie school graduate sells a Nissan to a banker. This cynical cycle was then perpetuated by the leaders that followed him. The upshot of such shallow (albeit effective) means of persuasion is that the American mind, over time, has come to regard politics as if it were some form of consumer-oriented entertainment. But popular entertainment, as Bernays said himself, "is the greatest unconscious carrier of propaganda in the world today. It is a great distributor for ideas and opinions. . . . Because pictures are made to meet market demands, they reflect, emphasize and even exaggerate broad popular tendencies, rather than stimulate new ideas and opinions."[255]

The Founders did not intend for the politician to be assigned a role in a theatrical production; instead, like the poet, the politician must practice the art of persuasion in order to discover the common good. His leverage must rest on the reasonableness of his conclusions, not on the scope of his influence. In this sense, the politician's responsibilities are similar to those of a judge. Each must identify the competing definitions of justice (and injustice) within in a complex situation and then craft a law that will discharge justice accordingly, both in the instant case and all similar cases going forward. A law, therefore, can be rightly understood as a rule of reason directed to the common good. It is here we find the truth behind the "social contract" that binds democratic representatives to their constituents: the citizens surrender their individual rights to their representatives, who in turn agree to abide by the process of deliberation and the rules of reason.

This art of political persuasion is an arduous mental

exercise; one that requires immersion in the practical and abstract elements of Platonic dialogue. Through this process, the politician may come to expose the sophistry and special interests that cripple society's pursuit of the common good. This vigorous form of reasoning is not intended to be a pleasant foxtrot carried out by naïve persons of good intention; to the contrary, it is the most difficult and energetic task known to political statecraft.

As but one example, consider the gravity of the challenges faced by President Lincoln when he took office on March 4, 1861, by which point seven states had already seceded from the Union. As historian William Miller writes, the political questions facing Lincoln were of existential importance:

> Could he discern objectively, not deceiving himself with wishes, the actual shape of the concrete reality in which he would make decisions? Could he connect the great moral principles to which he had given voice to the severely limiting realities of the actual complicated world he faced? Having made that discernment and that connection, could he *decide*? Or would he, like Buchanan, postpone, procrastinate, and waver? Having decided, could he persuade others?

> Could he lead? Having decided and persuaded, could he hold to his course through vicissitudes? But could he then change—admit mistakes, alter course—when circumstances would warrant?[256]

In this most taxing of enterprises, the politician's role is one of discipline, not performance. The representative's great assignment is to learn and relearn the common good and by means of legislation teach it to future generations of citizens. Only then may liberty and justice truly be achieved.

* * *

Gustave Flaubert once wrote that "by dint of railing at idiots, one runs the risk of become idiotic oneself." I appear to have fallen into this trap. Nevertheless, being aware as I am of Orwell's criticism of Dickens, I have done my best to find a solution to our predicament. And I believe, firmly and optimistically, that the solution lies in the famous words of German mathematician Carl Jacobi: *man muss immer umkehren*, or, loosely translated, "invert, always invert."

Propaganda teaches us to accept as obvious what is reasonable to doubt. According to Jacobi's law of inversion, we must solve the problem of propaganda by restating the meaning of propaganda in its inverse form. So, the question must be: What teaches us to doubt what may seem obvious to us? The answer, it seems to me, is reason. Reason, as history shows us, can and must rule. And I believe, as Robert Kennedy did, that "we are brave enough to be told the truth of where we stand."

4
THE ART OF THE POSSIBLE

"Choose confrontation wisely, but when it is your time don't be afraid to stand up, speak up, and speak out against injustice. And if you follow your truth down road to peace and the affirmation of love, if you shine like a beacon for all to see, then the poetry of all the great dreamers and philosophers is yours to manifest in a nation, a world community, and a Beloved Community that is finally at peace with itself."

John Lewis

Thus far I have been indulging, in perhaps disorderly fashion, in the tragicomic art of describing politicians and wealthy capitalists—who struggle to govern and manage themselves—as better or worse than they are. This is inevitable if politics is, as I am saying it is, at bottom the art of persuasion, which can be violent at one extreme, rational at the other, and variously both in between. So bear in mind that I do not cite the aforementioned persons in order to indict them; rather I use them as diagnostic probes to detect and understand the troubles that lie at the heart of American democracy. Make no mistake, the antics of the extreme right must be attended to as the Romans once attended to the quacking geese on Capitoline Hill; but I firmly believe that the majority of Americans are capable of acting with malice toward none, with charity for all, and uniting together in pursuit of the common good.

Before suggesting a path forward, however, it was necessary to first outline the various equations that pull our country's organizational and psychological strings. As Dr. King said, "in order to answer the question, 'Where do we go from here?' which is our theme, we must first honestly recognize where we are now."[257] At this point, I hope a few things are evident: (1) advertising *is* propaganda; they are synonymous; (2) we have long been blind to the power of propaganda, which is not surprising given its purpose; (3) most politicians are beholden, consciously or otherwise, to private interests; and (4) private power has increased while public consent has withered. How, then, are we to solve these myriad problems?

The answer to our predicament, I propose, is found in the source of persuasion provided to us by the Founders: The First Amendment. Despite its seeming clarity, however, the First Amendment has a curious and complex history. To understand its application in American society, it is useful to provide a brief history of the "common law" and its role in American jurisprudence.

Much has been written on the history of common law, but suffice it to say that the common law, as traditionally understood, is essentially tantamount to private law—it governs one's private interactions in civil society.* The common law system has its origins in England of the Middle Ages, and its basic elements are quite simple. A man gets a reputation in his community for fairness and wisdom. When a dispute arises between two or more of his neighbors, they come to him and present their arguments (i.e., their case) and wait for his neutral and detached opinion. Over time, as the man judges more cases and issues more opinions, he begins to assemble the connections, similarities, and differences among the various cases into a general body of principles by which future disputes can be resolved. This broad set of principles then operates as the starting point for settling novel disputes, the resolutions of

* Unless otherwise noted, I draw much of what I write here from the brilliant Scott Buchanan, *So Reason Can Rule*, 105-184 (1958).

which are incorporated into the same body of law. The "common law," therefore, is equally binding and tentative; it governs one's conduct within a community but remains subject to modification as new situations arise. To this day, it persists as the foundation of community life; human behavior is deemed lawful only insofar as it conforms to the principles of common law.

For educational purposes, the common law is divided into four topics: crime, property, contracts, and torts. Oliver Wendell Holmes, in his book *Common Law*, discusses each of the four divisions as having a common genesis. According to Holmes, human beings tend to interpret other people's conduct as wrongs committed against them. They then seek to right these wrongs by inflicting punishment against the alleged wrongdoer. Under the common law system, the degree of punishment is decided through the courts via the act of reason, and these reasons, with the help of judges, become enshrined in law once the case is adjudicated. If need be, the rules can be reversed or adjusted after the presentation of a new case, thus allowing for a continuing process of refinement. As Lord Mansfield famously said, the common law "works itself pure."[258]

The common law, very simply stated, encourages and protects citizens in their private pursuits of happiness. The citizen contributes to the law and then must abide by his contribution, avoiding harm to others in the process. Such general principles correspond to the familiar doctrines of free will and freedom—each person has the capacity as well as the right to conduct himself as he sees fit so long as his conduct does not interfere with the rights of others.

Against this backdrop, it can be seen that the common law provides the operational foundations for the system of free enterprise. Criminal law and the law of torts safeguard the operations of the market, the factory, and the bank, all of which transact business according to the rules of property and contract. Over time, these common-law bundles of freedom have blossomed into concentrations of power that are now recognized as institutions bearing public burdens, or "incorporations." The corporation defends itself from "government interference" because as a private, profit-seeking actor, it believes that the best government is that which governs least.

This mindset reveals itself clearly in the form of Vice President Michael R. Pence. As Governor of Indiana, Pence, in 2016, signed the repeal of an 80-year-old state law that set a minimum wage for most state construction projects. His reason? "Wages on public projects should be *set by the marketplace* and not by government bureaucracy" (emphasis mine).[259] It is clear that Pence's voice is that of the common man trained in the habits of common law. For him, "freedom" is synonymous with immunity from interference. Thus the market—where freedom flourishes for the common man—is to be regarded as the model of free society. As an additional example of this mindset, Pence published a poorly written essay in 2000 in which he argued that "smoking doesn't kill. In fact, two out of every three smokers doesn't [sic] die from a smoking-related illness." For the unprincipled Pence, "big government disguised as do-gooder, healthcare rhetoric" is a greater "scourge" than cancer. Pence's hero, in his own words, is naturally Ronald Reagan.[260]

In the courts, the First Amendment is, broadly speaking, interpreted as a common law (i.e., private law) doctrine. Since speech, press, assembly, petition, and religion increasingly involve private disputes regarding property ownership or contractual obligations, the First Amendment is often interpreted from the vantage point of the market. Justice Holmes almost certainly had this reading of the First Amendment in mind when he wrote his dissenting opinion in *Abrams v. United States* (1919), where he opined "that the best test of truth is the power of the thought *to get itself accepted in the competition of the market,* and that truth is the only ground upon which [citizens'] wishes safely can be carried out" (emphasis mine).

Holmes's famous "marketplace of ideas" metaphor has dominated Supreme Court jurisprudence over the past century. One recent study found that the term was used in 125 opinions between 1919 and 1995 by 24 of the 49 Justices who served on the Court for at least one year.[261] And nearly 80 percent of those opinions were written after 1970.

It therefore is not hyperbole to say that Holmes's market-based principle has influenced every single area of First Amendment jurisprudence: campaign spending, commercial speech, protest demonstrations, speech at schools and universities, libel, picketing, privacy, broadcasting, freedom of the press, obscenity, and freedom of speech.[262] Very summarily stated, this reading of the First Amendment holds that civil liberties are to be left in the realm of private law—they are regarded as "privileges" in the most literal sense. The Holmesian interpretation of the First Amendment naturally dovetails with a strict interpretation of the classical notion of limited government. Because the First Amendment's privileges are rooted in private conduct, it follows that *res publica* (the republic or "public thing"), should never invade them.

The Supreme Court's remarkably regressive decision in *Citizens United v. Federal Election Commission* was, of course, based in part on the "marketplace of ideas" principle. There, the Court ruled that the "government may not, under the First Amendment, suppress political speech on the basis of the speaker's corporate identity." Viewing Holmes's idea literally rather than metaphorically, the Court reasoned that because political speech takes place in the marketplace, then participants *within* the market—including corporations—necessarily have a constitutional right to engage in political speech. "All speakers," the Court wrote, "including individuals and the media, use money amassed from the economic marketplace to *fund their speech,* and the First Amendment protects the resulting speech" (emphasis mine). For the Court, speech is funded, not spoken. It draws no distinction between the rhetoric of a salesman and the rhetoric of the political forum. The same is true for America writ large.*

Persuasion depends on power. And the power of persuasion—due to the influence of Holmes's marketplace-of-ideas principle—is found in the private sphere. It resets upon the notion that an idea is only true to the extent that it fits within the prevailing set of market ideas. Persuasion and deliberation, as a result, are reduced to the most superficial means possible: wealth. And wealth, unlike speech, cannot be heard. It lingers in the darkness of ambiguity and diversion and reveals itself to us only in its final form: the law. "Dark money" in this sense is not so much hyperbole as it is an accurate description of the market's power. The market's biggest "influencers" hide their power in the pockets of politicians and then shield their identities under the guise of the First Amendment. Politicians, in turn, confuse thought with propaganda and deals with consent, and then use corporate money to ensure reelection and perpetuate prestige. Threat and seclusion

* President Obama, a constitutional scholar, readily recognized the danger of the Supreme Court's decision, stating in his 2010 State of the Union address that it "will open the floodgates for special interests—including foreign corporations—to spend without limit in our elections."

have consequently taken the place of reason and inclusion. Dark money; shadow headquarters; closed-door fundraisers; Bernagie political influence—these are the powers of the First Amendment today. For Teddy Roosevelt, this situation would be regarded as "the corruption of the electorate."[263] Today, it is called "speech."

* * *

Remembering Jacobi's words, we must invert the current definition of the First Amendment in order to reclaim its power. Or as Dr. King said, we must "cause the oppressor to become ashamed of his own methods."[264] As citizens, our First Amendment must be positive and open; it must prosper under the light of rational persuasion so that the necessary social, economic, and bureaucratic processes may come to bear their share of the burden for justice and injustice. By embarking on this quest together, we will come to understand that there are more undiscovered ends in public life than the philosophy of private freedom could ever dream of.

Abraham Lincoln defined the function of government as follows: "The legitimate object of government is to do for the community of people whatever they need to have done, but cannot do at all, or cannot so well do, for themselves, in their separate and individual capacities." As set forth in the Preamble of the Constitution, that what needs to be done for the people, but cannot be done at all or as well by individual effort, is the attainment of the common good, specifically: union, justice, liberty, tranquility, common defense, and general welfare—the latter two clearly extrapolations from the first four. The plain language of the Constitution makes painfully apparent that the Founders did not see government as a business; instead, as Lincoln recognized, government is interested only in union, justice, liberty, and tranquility, all of which come together to form the common good. Persuasion that does not reach this level of abstraction should fail.

The means for achieving the common good are found in the First Amendment: speech, press, assembly, and religion. As citizens, we must recognize that the tools embedded within the First Amendment are not privileges but *duties*; in the words of Jane Addams, "it will be impossible" to foster "a higher civic life" unless we do so "through common intercourse."[265] This is the reason why the First Amendment exists. The Founders' grand innovation was to transform the private individual, the *idiote* as the Greeks called him, into a public actor. Recalling the pride of the Romans in the ancient *res publica,* the Founders conferred on the private individual a public title: *citizen*—the first official title in the public realm. The First Amendment, interpreted as the recognition by the government of its obligations to protect and support certain activities of the citizen, suggests that the primary functions of the citizen are speech, press, assembly, and religion. They are the means by which injustice can be recognized and justice can be achieved. Unlike Holmes and his disciples, who regard the First Amendment as if Lincoln had once said "government of the corporation, by the corporation, for the corporation, shall not perish from the earth," we as citizens must interpret the First Amendment from the vantage point of the public good—what needs to be done by the people, for the people.

To see how the First Amendment can be utilized to achieve the common good, we must study history; in the words of the great Congressman and Civil Rights champion, John Lewis, "it is unlikely that what [we] hope to accomplish is new." By studying history's various masters in the art of persuasion, we can see that, to a person, each First Amendment advocate persuaded their fellow citizens to pursue a new vision for America by embracing the perambulatory language of the common good.

Frederick Douglass, whom Elizabeth Cady Stanton described as a "majestic" orator due to the "wondrous gifts of his pathos and humor," fought the evils of slavery by embracing the Constitution's perambulatory purpose. In his famous "Fifth of July Speech" in 1852, Douglass proclaimed:

> Fellow-citizens! There is no matter in respect to which, the people of the North

> have allowed themselves to be so ruinously imposed upon, as that of the pro-slavery character of the Constitution. In that instrument I hold there is no warrant, license, nor sanction of the hateful thing; but, interpreted as it ought to be interpreted, the constitution is a GLORIOUS LIBERTY DOCUMENT. Read its preamble, consider its purposes. Is slavery among them? Is it at the gateway? or is it in the temple? it is neither. . . . I hold that every American citizen has a right to form an opinion of the constitution, and to propagate that opinion, and to use all honorable means to make his opinion the prevailing one. With out this right, the liberty of an American citizen would be as insecure as that of a Frenchman.[266]

Martin Luther King, a student of history, learned from Douglass that the Constitution's definition of the common good provided an immense source of persuasive power. The Emancipation Proclamation, said King, was "the one moment in the country's history when a bold, brave *start* had been made, and a redirection to the obvious fact that urgent business was at hand—the resolution of that noble journey toward the goals reflected in the Preamble to the

Constitution."[267]

Susan B. Anthony, who along with Elizabeth Cady Stanton was the nineteenth century's torchbearer of the women's suffrage movement, likewise relied upon the Constitution's perambulatory definition of the common good to persuade America to embrace gender equality. After being arrested for casting an illegal vote in the presidential election of 1872, Anthony stood before her fellow citizens and embarked on an effort "to *prove*" (emphasis mine) that she "committed no crime, but instead simply exercised my citizen's rights, guaranteed to me and all United States citizens by the National Constitution, beyond the power of any state to deny." Citing "the preamble of the Federal Constitution," Anthony maintained that it was "we, the *whole* people, who formed the Union. And we formed it, not to give the blessings of liberty, but to *secure* them; not to the half of ourselves and the half of our posterity, but to the *whole* people—women as well as men." And because "Webster, Worcester, and Bouvier all define a *citizen* to be a *person* in the United States, entitled to vote and hold office," then, by virtue of logic, "the only question left to be settled now is: Are women persons? And I hardly believe any of our opponents will have the hardihood to say they are not. Being persons, then, women are citizens; and no state has a right to make any law, or to enforce any old law, that shall abridge their privileges or immunities."[268]

Congresswoman Barbara Jordan's speech during

the Nixon impeachment proceedings remains enshrined in the halls of history. She began by noting that although the Constitution had once excluded her from its protections, President Nixon would not face a more devoted defender of the Constitution's perambulatory purpose:

> Earlier today, we heard the beginning of the Preamble to the Constitution of the United States: "We, the people." It's a very eloquent beginning. But when that document was completed on the seventeenth of September in 1787, I was not included in that "We, the people." I felt somehow for many years that George Washington and Alexander Hamilton just left me out by mistake. But through the process of amendment, interpretation, and court decision, I have finally been included in "We, the people."
>
> Today I am an inquisitor. An hyperbole would not be fictional and would not overstate the solemnness that I feel right now. My faith in the Constitution is whole; it is complete; it is total. And I am not going to sit here and be an idle spectator to the diminution, the

> subversion, the destruction, of the Constitution.

Two years later, in 1976, Representative Jordan became the first African American woman to deliver the keynote address at the Democratic National Convention. Naturally, she used her platform to persuade citizens and public servants alike to rededicate themselves to the common good:

> A nation is formed by the willingness of each of us to share in the responsibility for upholding the common good. A government is invigorated when each one of us is willing to participate in shaping the future of this nation. In this election year, we must define the "common good" and begin again to shape a common future. Let each person do his or her part. If one citizen is unwilling to participate, all of us are going to suffer. For the American idea, though it is shared by all of us, is realized in each one of us.
>
> And now, what are those of us who are elected public officials supposed to do? We call ourselves "public servants" but I'll tell you this: We as public servants

> must set an example for the rest of the nation. It is hypocritical for the public official to admonish and exhort the people to uphold the common good if we are derelict in upholding the common good. More is required—More is required of public officials than slogans and handshakes and press releases. More is required. We must hold ourselves strictly accountable. We must provide the people with a vision of the future.[269]

Eleanor Roosevelt, during her celebrated "Struggle for Human Rights" speech before the United Nations in 1948, addressed "one of the greatest issues of our time—that is the preservation of human freedom." Citing the recent atrocities committed by totalitarian systems of government, Roosevelt called on all nations to recognize that "the propaganda we have witnessed in the recent past, like that we perceive in these days, seeks to impugn, to undermine, and to destroy the liberty and independence of peoples." "Among free men," Roosevelt declared, "the end cannot justify the means. We know the patterns of totalitarianism—the single political party, the control of schools, press, radio, the arts, the sciences, and the church to support autocratic authority; these are the age-old patterns against which men have struggled for three thousand years." To guard against these dangers, "there must always be consideration of the rights of others." "But," Roosevelt clarified, "in a democracy this is not a restriction. Indeed, in our democracies we make our freedoms secure because each of us is expected to respect the rights of others and we are free to make our own laws. Freedom for our peoples is not only a right, but also a tool. *Freedom of speech, freedom of the press, freedom of information, freedom of assembly—these are not just abstract ideals to us; they are tools with which we create a way of life, a way of life in which we can enjoy freedom*" (emphasis mine).[270]

Going forward, we must adhere to the model of progress so beautifully articulated by Eleanor Roosevelt: "Freedom of speech, freedom of the press, freedom of information, freedom of assembly—these are not just abstract ideals to us; they are tools with which we create a way of life, a way of life in which we can enjoy freedom." As citizens, the First Amendment is *our* tool of persuasion. The Founders bestowed upon *us*, the *citizens*, a public duty to pursue the common good. The corporation, the *idiote*, the Bernagie thinker—they have failed us. For too long we have sat in the darkness of Plato's cave and assumed that our reality is governed by the shadows. We must take back our reverence and love of nature and move beyond our shrewd ingenuities in exploiting it. We must commit ourselves to a public philosophy of citizenship. We must replace opinion and power with reason and truth. We must purge the hate and injustice of the current age and replace it with the love and justice of the new. We must exhibit prudent judgment and sound integrity. We must value not luxury but liberty; not celebrity but community; not selfishness but sacrifice.

* * *

Some have said that, in today's complex world, progress is not found in politics. Indeed studies show that my generation, the Millennials, regard business leaders, not political leaders, as the chieftains of progress.[271] If we remain fixed to our current reality, then perhaps that will prove true. Our government today is futile and openly hostile to processes of justice. Technological novelty has yielded political rigidity and polarization. This is what Thoreau meant when he said, "Improved means to an unimproved end."[272] In such times, the dogmatic adherence to political custom, coupled with a studied unwillingness to change course, may very well ignite a rapid accumulation of injustices, not only in the current political cycle but in the foreseeable future as well. If we continue on our current path, the political will to create justice-oriented laws and institutions will be replaced by the habit of domination on the part of domineering authorities. Reason will give way to force, and legality will take on the sinister meaning of *law and order*.

It is in such circumstances that the citizen must

rediscover not only his right but his *duty* of revolution. The tools of persuasion must be taken from the powers that be so that justice may be restored. Revolution, as the Founders taught us, is a necessary condition of effective and responsible government.

The use of the word "revolution" perhaps causes apprehension. It is true that, as commonly used, the term is applied to technological developments, as in the "Industrial Revolution," when a term like *evolution* would be more accurate. It is also true that revolution is identified with any attempt to overthrow a body of government. But this once again misses the essential nature of the term revolution as properly understood. The revolutionary path should never be confused with the replacement of a mechanical part or the swapping of a constitution. A revolution is grounded above all in truth and justice. "The real American Revolution," wrote John Adams in 1818, took place "in the minds and hearts of the people." And real revolutions "ought never to be undertaken rashly; nor without deliberate consideration and sober reflection; nor without a solid, immutable, eternal foundation of justice and humanity; nor without a people possessed of intelligence, fortitude, and integrity sufficient to carry them with steadiness, patience, and perseverance, through all the vicissitudes of fortune, the fiery trials and melancholy disasters they may have to encounter."[273]

A starting point in our revolutionary quest for justice would be to examine the teachings of Socrates.

The wisdom of Socrates was that he did not proclaim to know what he did not know. The foolish man, by contrast, thinks he knows when he does not know; doesn't know that he does not know; and has no suspicion of what he does not know. The foolish man may be anything from an artist to a politician. And all of them, Socrates says, are potential tyrants. These human beings are the prisoners in the depth of the cave who are fascinated and enslaved by the shadows, so much so that they have learned to trace, correlate, and even predict the shadows' movements. Socrates was shocked when he discovered this ignorance. But he was able to convey his shock to the shockers. He did so by relentlessly questioning their beliefs and assumptions, aiming not to embarrass those to whom he spoke but to create a genuine sense of self-awareness. "Men of Athens," he pleaded during his trial for impiety and corruption in 399 BC, "I care for and love you, . . . and while I have life and strength I shall *never* cease from the practice and teaching of philosophy, exhorting and expostulating with any one of you whom I meet and saying to him in my usual manner: 'You, my friend—a citizen of the great city of Athens, famous for its culture and power—are you not ashamed of heaping up the largest amount of money and status and reputation, and caring so little about wisdom and truth and improving as much as possible your soul, which you never regard or heed at all?"[274]

Socrates was the first to admit that he did not have

all of the answers to life's problems, but he firmly believed that the common good could be secured only through reasoned inquiry and the pursuit of knowledge. "We shall be better and braver and less helpless," Socrates told Meno, "if we think that we ought to enquire, than we should have been if we indulged in the idle fancy that there was no knowing and no use in seeking to know what we do not know—that is a theme upon which I am ready to fight, in word and deed, to the utmost of my power."[275]

Socrates provided to us a model for achieving the common good. A great awakening requires persistent questioning. This process of inquiry must be undertaken not to humiliate, but to enlighten. Martin Luther King combined Socratic reasoning with Gandhi's philosophy of non-violence to create a unique Kingsian philosophy of love and progress. And through this process he was able to convince America to *care* about racism. "The majority of white America consider themselves sincerely committed to justice for the Negro," he wrote. "But unfortunately this is a fantasy of self-deception and comfortable vanity. Overwhelmingly America is still struggling with irresolution and contradiction. It has been sincere and even ardent in welcoming some change. But too quickly apathy and disinterest rise to the surface when the next logical steps are to be taken."[276] It was for this reason that "Negroes united and marched. And out of the new unity and action vast monuments of dignity were shaped, courage was forged and hope took concrete form."[277] The non-violence movement, as Dr. King learned from Gandhi's practice of *satyagraha*, maximized reason by minimizing force, thus allowing truth to be spoken to power. Civil rights leaders grabbed hold of the First Amendment to ignite a public discussion about the things that need to be done, but cannot be done, by individual effort—the objective of democratic government, as Lincoln tells us. The byproduct of their monumental efforts was true justice, enshrined in law: the Civil Rights Act; the Economic Opportunity Act; the Foot Stamp Act; the Higher Education Act; the Voting Rights Act; the Elementary and Secondary Education Act; the Department of Housing and Urban Development Act, among others. All of the Great Society bills were passed in two-year period because the country had been forced, by persuasion grounded in reason, to confront the myriad social problems that led to inequality and injustice. "The real hero of this struggle," President Lyndon Johnson declared in 1965, "is the American Negro. His actions and protests, his courage to risk safety and even to risk his life, have awakened the conscience of this Nation. His demonstrations have been designed to call attention to injustice, designed to provoke change, designed to stir reform. He has called upon us to make good the promise of America. And who among us can say that we would have made the same progress were it not for his persistent bravery, and his faith in American democracy."[278]

Socrates teaches us that we must ask questions to achieve justice. Now we must rediscover which questions to ask. Once again, the Founders have provided us with the answer: If the people are "not enlightened enough to exercise their control with wholesome discretion," wrote Jefferson, "the remedy is not to take it from them, but to inform their discretion by education. This is the true corrective of abuses of constitutional power."[279] John Adams agreed: "All sober inquirers after truth, ancient and modern, pagan and Christian, have declared that the happiness of man, as well as his dignity, consists in virtue." Therefore, wrote Adams, a "liberal education" must be undertaken to "enlighten the people's understandings and improve their morals . . . to enable them to comprehend the scheme of government, and to know upon what points their liberties depend; to dissipate those vulgar prejudices and popular superstitions that oppose themselves to good government; and to teach them that obedience to the laws is as indispensable in them as in lords and kings."[280]

I can attest first-hand to the power of a liberal arts education. I attended Dickinson College, a small liberal arts school in Carlisle, Pennsylvania. The school was chartered on September 9, 1783, six days after the Treaty of Paris, making it the first college to be founded after the formation of the United States. Its founder was one of *the* Founders, Dr. Benjamin Rush, who named the school after the "Penman of the Revolution," John Dickinson—a signer of the Constitution whose fame in colonial America stemmed from his publication of 12 *Letters from a Farmer in Pennsylvania* in 1767-1768. "A more estimable man," Thomas Jefferson wrote of Dickinson shortly after his death, "or truer patriot, could not have left us. Among the first of the advocates for the rights of his country when assailed by Great Britain, he continued to the last the orthodox advocate of the true principles of our new government: and his name will be consecrated in history as one of the great worthies of the revolution."[281] The school's motto, fashioned in the spirit of the Founders, is *Pietate et doctrina tuta libertas*: "Freedom is made safe through character and learning."[282]

It was at Dickinson that I came to see that an unexamined life is not worth living. From Emerson, I learned of *Man Thinking*. From Du Bois, I learned of life within the veil. From Lao Tzu, I learned the Way. From Aeschylus, I learned tragedy. From Aristophanes, I learned comedy. From Aristotle, I learned *eudaimonia*. From Nietzsche, I learned *amor fati*. From Kant, I learned the imperative. From Hegel, I learned growth. From Descartes, I learned nothing. From Twain, I learned irony. From Truth, I learned hope. From Sinclair, I learned legislation. From Frost, I learned limitations. From Morrison, I learned beauty.

I could go on and on. But above all, what Dickinson showed me was that learning is *fun*. There is a legitimate sense of awe that comes with achieving self-awareness; you can feel your psyche transforming in real time. As Adams wrote, the process of learning is "truly sublime and astonishing."[283] I was grateful for the opportunity to have my beliefs challenged and my shortcomings exposed. I enjoyed the freedom of open discourse. I relished in the experience of sitting down with a book and *feeling* the emotions of a protagonist. And through the processes of learning and conversing with friends and professors alike—what Alfred North Whitehead called the "adventure of ideas"—I gained a true appreciation for the wonder of mankind. My education was, in a very real sense, enlightening.

The Founders prioritized the liberal arts because a liberal arts education teaches us that the pursuit of happiness is synonymous with the public good. "No phase except 'liberty,'" writes historian Gordon Wood, "was invoked more often by the revolutionaries than the 'public good.' It expressed the colonists' deepest hatreds of the old order and their most visionary hopes for a new day."[284]

I believe that our generation can be the public good generation. We can bring to the public sphere a true philosophy of citizenship, one that subscribes not to the slogan of "every man for himself" but rather to the maxim of "all for the common cause." As Thomas Paine wrote centuries ago, "We have it in our power to begin the world over again."[285] I am convinced that there remains a vital core within mankind that would rather travel the arduous path of justice than the reassuring path of comfort; that would rather suffer agony in the quest for peace than sit with ease in the shadow of the cave; that would rather engage in the rigor of critical thinking than seek solace in the luxury of material goods. I believe that the majority of Americans long for a more mature, educated citizenry that seeks knowledge in books, understanding in the execution of civic duty, and a sense of purpose in the pursuit of the common good.

But I must reiterate the urgency with which we must act. As Dr. King said, "there is such thing as being too late. Procrastination is still the thief of time. Life often leaves us standing bare, naked and dejected with a lost opportunity."[286] We cannot allow history to one day look down upon our generation and describe our efforts in the most pathetic words of, "they tried, but alas, they were too late."

We must prove to the Founders that reason can rule. Trust that we have the ability. We can persuade by proof rather than influence. We can engage in rational debate. We can seek truth without fear of repercussion. We can love our community more than our capital. We can be poets *and* public servants. We can recognize our mistakes with forbearance. We can lead not by authority but by principle. We can forgive with compassion. We can respond to novelty with flexibility. We can examine the past to plan our future. We can embrace tradition *and* diversity. We can hope for more than hope. We can have the audacity to fight for justice. And in the final analysis, perhaps we can look back upon our efforts and say proudly, we are the New Generation—humbled by life's lessons, patient in times of tribulation, guided by hope in the future, imbued with a spirit of service, and, most of all, dedicated to the pursuit of a great ideal.

ABOUT THE AUTHOR

Thomas F. Brier, Jr., is a native of Hershey, Pennsylvania. He attended Dickinson College, where he played basketball, fell in love with The Wire, and graduated with a degree in Philosophy. He earned his Juris Doctor in 2017 from Penn State Law, where he was elected commencement speaker by his classmates. After graduation, he served as a law clerk on the U.S. Court of Appeals for the Third Circuit. He is currently working as an Associate at Blank Rome LLP in Philadelphia.

NOTE ABOUT THE COVER

The cover is modeled after Francisco Goya's 1799 etching, "The Sleep of Reason Produces Monsters." Goya imagines himself asleep amidst his drawing tools, his reason dulled by slumber and bedeviled by creatures that prowl in the dark. The work includes owls that may be symbols of folly and bats symbolizing ignorance. Goya's nightmare reflected his view of Spanish society, which he portrayed as demented, corrupt, and ripe for ridicule. The full epigraph, No. 43 in *Los Caprichos,* reads: "Fantasy abandoned by reason produces impossible monsters: united with her (reason), she (fantasy) is the mother of the arts and the origin of their marvels."

End Notes (Author's Note: I did my best to cite all references in this book. All citation mistakes are mine alone. And my apologies for the lack of a uniform citation method. The Bluebook has forever doomed my citation capacities.)

---

[1] William Stevenson, *A Man Called Intrepid* 159-162 (1976). Churchill's dilemma at Coventry has appeared in various texts over the years (see, e.g., F. W. Winterbotham, *The Ultra Secret* (1974) and Cave Brown, *Bodyguard of Lies* (1974)), but the story has also been disputed on the ground that the encryption reports did not reveal the specific location of the next raid. Churchill's paid biographer has asserted the latter view. Nevertheless, while the historical accounts differ, the story perfectly illustrates the existential nature of the dilemmas that often arise during wartime.

[2]Rahwan, Iyad. "What Moral Decisions Should Driverless Cars Make?" *TED: Ideas Worth Spreading*, Sept. 2016, www.ted.com/talks/iyad_rahwan_what_moral_decisions_should_driverless_cars_make/discussion?ref=hvper.com.

[3] Galeon, Dom and Reedy, Christianna. "Kurzweil Claims That the Singularity Will Happen by 2045," *Futurism,* October 5, 2017, https://futurism.com/kurzweil-claims-that-the-singularity-will-happen-by-2045/.

[4] Walter Isaacson, *Benjamin Franklin: An American Life* 449 (2004); Derek A. Webb, "The 'Spirit of Amity': The Constitution's cover letter and civic friendship, The Constitution Center, Dec. 13, 2012, https://constitutioncenter.org/blog/the-e2809cspirit-of-amitye2809d-the-constitutione28099s-cover-letter-and-ci.

[5] Aristotle, *The Politics*, Book 3, Chapter 9.

[6] Robert F. Kennedy, "Remarks at the University of Kansas," March 18, 1968, https://www.jfklibrary.org/Research/Research-Aids/Ready-Reference/RFK-Speeches/Remarks-of-Robert-F-Kennedy-at-the-University-of-Kansas-March-18-1968.aspx.

[7] David Hulme, "X-Risks and Human Destiny," Vision, September 2017, http://www.vision.org/martin-rees-interview-human-extinction-6594.

[8] Kaplan, Robert D. "Was Democracy Just a Moment?" *The Atlantic,* Atlantic Media Company, Dec. 1997, www.theatlantic.com/magazine/archive/1997/12/was-democracy-just-a-moment/306022/.

[9] Theodore Roosevelt, *Oliver Cromwell* 206, 223 (1900); Kaplan, *supra* note 8.

[10] Daron Acemoglu and James A. Robinson, *Why Nations Fail* 189-193 (2012).
[11] Bernard Bailyn, *The Ideological Origins of the American Revolution* 50 (1967).
[12] *Id.* at 25-26; Footnote: Robert Tombs, *The English and Their History*, 321 (2014).
[13] David McCullough, *John Adams* 121 (2001).
[14] Isaacson, *supra* note 4, at 25; Plutarch, *Poplicola trans John Dryden*, available at, https://constitution.org/rom/plutarch/poplicola.htm.
[15] Titus Livius (Livy), *The History of Rome, trans* George Baker, http://oll.libertyfund.org/titles/1754.
[16] Publius Cornelius Tacitus, *The Works of Tacitus*, vol. 1 (Gordon's Discourses, Annals (Books 1-3)), available at http://oll.libertyfund.org/titles/tacitus-the-works-of-tacitus-vol-1-gordons-discourses-annals-books-1-3
[17] Bernard Bailyn, *The Ideological Origins of the American Revolution* 27 (1967).
[18] Hector St. Jean de Crèvecœur, *Hector St. Jean de Crèvecœur Describes the American people,* 1782, http://www.americanyawp.com/reader/a-new-nation/hector-st-jean-de-crevecoeur-describes-the-american-people-1782/
[19] Joyce Appleby, et al., *Telling the Truth About History* 39 (1994).
[20] Thomas Hobbes, *Of Man, Being the First Part of Leviathan*, Chapter XIII, https://www.bartleby.com/34/5/13.html.
[21] Madison Debates, June 18, 1787, http://avalon.law.yale.edu/18th_century/debates_618.asp
[22] Govan, Thomas P. "The Rich, the Well-Born, and Alexander Hamilton." The Mississippi Valley Historical Review, vol. 36, no. 4, 1950, pp. 675–680. JSTOR, JSTOR, www.jstor.org/stable/1895524.
[23] *Federalist* (No. 55).
[24] Daniel Lambright, *Man, Morality, and the United States Constitution*, 17 U. Pa. J. Const. L. 1487, 1514 (2015).
[25] John Locke, "Essay Concerning Human Understanding," Book II, Chapter I.
[26] John Locke, "Second Treatise of Government," Chapter VII, § 87
[27] Id. § 88.
[28] Issacson, *supra* note 4, at 312.
[29] Scott Buchanan, *So Reason Can Rule* 33 (1982).
[30] Charles Louis de Secondat, Baron de Montesquieu, *The Sprit of Laws*, Chapters 4.5 and 5.3 (1748).
[31] Buchanan, *supra* note 39, at 56.

[32] *Id.* at 66.
[33] Michael J. Sandel, *Democracy's Discontent* 36-39 (1997); Eze, Ugonna. "The Anti-Federalists and Their Important Role during the Ratification Fight." *National Constitution Center*, constitutioncenter.org/blog/the-anti-federalists-and-their-important-role-during-the-ratification-fight.
[34] Richard Hofstadter, *The Age of Reform* 35-36 (1955).
[35] Gordon S. Wood, *The Radicalism of the American Revolution* 236 (1992).
[36] *Id.* at 190.
[37]James Wilson, *Lectures on Law*, (1790-91), http://global.oup.com/us/companion.websites/fdscontent/uscompanion/us/static/companion.websites/9780199751358/instructor/chapter_4/jameswilson.pdf.
[38] Wood, *supra* note 35, at 229.
[39] Susan Jacoby, *The Age of American Unreason* 35 (2008).
[40] The Founders' Constitution, Volume 1, Chapter 11, Document 10, Chicago University Press, http://press-pubs.uchicago.edu/founders/documents/v1ch11s10.html.
[41] Benjamin Franklin, "Proposals Relating to the Education of Youth in Pensilvania," 1749, University of Pennsylvania University Archives and Records Center, https://www.archives.upenn.edu/primdocs/1749proposals.html
[42] George Washington: "First Annual Address to Congress," January 8, 1790. Online by Gerhard Peters and John T. Woolley, *The American Presidency Project*. http://www.presidency.ucsb.edu/ws/?pid=29431.
[43] Allen, W.B., ed. George Washington: "A Collection; Washington, to the Commissioners of the District of Columbia," 143, 229, January 28, 1795. Indianapolis: Liberty Fund, 1988.
[44] Wood, *supra* note 35, at 216.
[45] *The Selected Writings of Benjamin Rush*. Edited by Dagobert D. Runes. New York: Philosophical Library, 1947, http://press-pubs.uchicago.edu/founders/documents/v1ch18s30.html
[46] Thomas Jefferson to Louis H. Girardin, 15 January 1815, Jefferson Papers, https://founders.archives.gov/documents/Jefferson/03-08-02-0167.
[47] Mark D. McGarvie, *Creating Roles for Religion and Philanthropy in A Secular Nation: The Dartmouth College Case and the Design of Civil Society in the Early Republic*, 25 J.C. & U.L. 527, 537-38 (1999).
[48] Wood, *supra* note 35, at 169.
[49] Carl Kaestle, *Pillars of the Republic: Common Schools and American Society, 1780-1860* 3, 546 (1983).
[50] Thomas Paine, *Rights of Man, Part the Second*, Chapter V, http://www.constitution.org/tp/rightsman2.htm.

[51] George Washington, "Farewell Address," 1796, The Avalon Project, http://avalon.law.yale.edu/18th_century/washing.asp
[52] Brackemyre, Ted. "Education to the Masses." *US History Scene*. 11 Apr. 2015. Web. 21 Aug. 2018.
[53] Bernard Manin, *The Principles of Representative Government* 111-12 (1997).
[54] Wood, *supra* note 35, at 259.
[55] Manin, *supra* note 53, at 114.
[56] Wood, *supra* note 35, at 266.
[57] Richard Hofstadter, *The Age of Reform* 25 (1955).
[58] See generally Mark D. McGarvie, *Creating Roles for Religion and Philanthropy in A Secular Nation: The Dartmouth College Case and the Design of Civil Society in the Early Republic*, 25 J.C. & U.L. 527 (1999).
[59] T. Pangle & L. Pangle, *The Learning of Liberty: The Educational Ideals of the American Founders* 118 (1992).
[60] Historically Black Colleges and Universities and Higher Education Desegregation, U.S. Department of Education, March 1991, https://www2.ed.gov/about/offices/list/ocr/docs/hq9511.html
[61] Eric Weiner, *The Geography of Genius, Man Seeks God* 26 (2016).
[62] Jacoby, *supra* note 39 at 55.
[63] Cecil B. Hayes, *The American Lyceum: Its History and Contribution to America*, 24 (1932), https://files.eric.ed.gov/fulltext/ED542227.pdf
[64] Jacoby, *supra* note 39 at 56.
[65] Alexis de Tocqueville, *Democracy in America, trans. Arthur Goldhammer* (New York: Library of America, 2004), 595–99.
[66] United States. Office of Education, Annual Report of the Commissioner of Education, Vol. I, 285-86 (1901).
[67] Susan Jacoby, *The Great Agnostic and the Golden Age of Freethought* 73-75, 159 (2004); Catherine H. Birney, *The Grimke Sisters* (1885), available at http://www.gutenberg.org/files/12044/12044-h/12044-h.htm
[68] Neil MacNeil, Richard A. Baker, *The American Senate: An Insider's History* 59 (2013).
[69] Merrill D. Peterson, *The Great Triumvirate: Webster, Clay, and Calhoun* 234 (1987).
[70] U.S. Senate, "Brief History of the Senate," https://www.senate.gov/artandhistory/history/idea_of_the_senate/1854Benton.htm.
[71] Johann N. Neem, *Democracy's Schools: The Rise of Public Education in America* 40 (2017).
[72] John Quincy Adams, "Lectures on Rhetoric and Oratory: Delivered to the Classes of Senior and Junior Sophisters in Harvard University,"Vol 1. Cambridge: Hilliard and Metcalf, 1810,

http://www.sjsu.edu/people/cynthia.rostankowski/courses/HUM2AF13/s3/Reader-Lecture-12-Adams-Grimke-Fell-Wollstonecraft.pdf

[73] Johann N. Neem, *Democracy's Schools: The Rise of Public Education in America* 50-51 (2017).

[74] Adams, *supra* note 72.

[75] Daniel J. Boorstin, *The Americans: The Democratic Experience* 462-67 (1973).

[76] Jacoby, *supra* note 39 at 8; Helen Dewar and Dana Milbank, "Cheney Dismisses Critic With Obscenity," *Washington Post*, June 25, 2004, http://www.washingtonpost.com/wp-dyn/articles/A3699-2004Jun24.html.

[77] Andrew Glass, "Speaker Reed reforms rules, Jan. 29, 1890," January 29, 2010, https://www.politico.com/story/2010/01/speaker-reed-reforms-rules-jan-29-1890-032175.

[78] James Grant, *Mr. Speaker!: The Life and Times of Thomas B. Reed - The Man Who Broke the Filibuster* 8 (2012).

[79] Albert Edward Winship, *Horace Mann: The Educator* 1-23 (1896); Dickson A. Mungazi, *The Evolution of Educational Theory in the United States* 186 (1999); Richard Miller Devens, Charles W. Chase, *The Glory of Our Yoith* 723 (1909); Massachusetts. Board of Education, Annual Report of the Board of Education (1838).

[80] Salomone, Rosemary C. (1996) "Common Schools, Uncommon Values: Listening to the Voices of Dissent," Yale Law & Policy Review: Vol. 14: Iss. 1, Article 5, http://digitalcommons.law.yale.edu/ylpr/vol14/iss1/5

[81] Horace Mann, *Lectures on Education*, 15 (1845).

[82] The R.I. Schoolmaster, Volume 17 (1871), https://books.google.com/books?id=a8AXAQAAIAAJ&printsec=frontcover&dq=editions:q5LMMvqAUi8C&hl=en&sa=X&ved=0ahUKEwijhv7jpf7cAhVqs1kKHeIRC-4Q6AEILjAB#v=onepage&q&f=false.

[83] *Id.*

[84] Salomone, *supra* note 80 at 174.

[85] Antioch College, "Life in the Community," http://www.antiochcollege.edu/campus_life/community

[86] *Addresses and Proceedings - National Education Association of the United States*, Volume 35, 67-68 (1896).

[87] The Landscape of Public Education, Educational Policy Institute, April 2011, http://www.educationalpolicy.org/publications/EPI%20Center/EPICenter_K-12.pdf.

[88] Joyce Appleby, *The Relentless Revolution: A History of Capitalism* 175 (2010).

[89] Boorstin, *supra* note 75, at 168-71.
[90] Johann N. Neem, *Democracy's Schools: The Rise of Public Education in America* 21-28 (2017).
[91] Salomone, *supra* note 80 at 175.
[92] James W. Fraser, *Between Church and State: Religion and Public Education in a Multicultural America* 27 (1999).
[93] Damon Mayrl, *Secular Conversions: Political Institutions and Religious Education in the United States and Australia,* 1800–2000, 52 (2016).
[94] Michael Dehaven Newsom, *Common School Religion: Judicial Narratives in A Protestant Empire,* 11 S. Cal. Interdisc. L.J. 219, 236 (2002) (quoting William Kailer Dunn, *What Happened to Religious Education?: The Decline of Religious Teaching in the Public Elementary School, 1776-1861*, 259 (1958)).
[95] Fraser, *supra* note 92 at 33.
[96] Boorstin, *supra* note 75, at 249.
[97] Newsom, *supra* note 92 at 242.
[98] The Church of St. Philip Neri, "The Nativist Riots," 2006, https://web.archive.org/web/20070822112107/http://churchofstphilipneri.org/history/NATIVIST%20RIOTS.pdf.
[99] Archdiocese of Philadelphia, "History," https://web.archive.org/web/20080509053947/http://catholicschools-phl.org/about/history.htm.
[100] Wilfred M. McClay, *Figures in the Carpet: Finding the Human Person in the American Past* 401 (2007).
[101] Richard Hofstadter, *Anti-Intellectualism in American Life* 157 (1963).
[102] *Id.* at 158.
[103] Steven Inskeep, "Donald Trump and the Legacy of Andrew Jackson," *The Atlantic,* Nov. 30, 2016, https://www.theatlantic.com/politics/archive/2016/11/trump-and-andrew-jackson/508973/; Fred Kaplan, *John Quincy Adams: American Visionary* 391 (2014).
[104] Hofstadter, *supra* note 57 at 44-46.
[105] Kaplan, *supra* note 103, at 428-33.
[106] Hofstadter, *supra* note 101 at 160.
[107] *Id.* at 159.
[108] Neem, *supra* note 90 at 32-33.
[109] Hofstadter, *supra* note 57 at 53-58.
[110] Hofstadter, *supra* note 57 at 135-36.
[111] Henry Adams, *The Education of Henry Adams*, Chapter 2, http://www.gutenberg.org/cache/epub/2044/pg2044.txt.
[112] Joyce Appleby, *The Relentless Revolution: A History of Capitalism* 175 (2010); William Leach, *Land of Desire: Merchants, Power, and the Rise of a New American Culture* 8 (1993).

[113] Leach, *supra* note 112, at 8.
[114] Hofstadter, *supra* note 57 at 136.
[115] *Id.* at 174; U.S. Census Bureau, "1910 Fast Facts," https://www.census.gov/history/www/through_the_decades/fast_facts/1910_fast_facts.html.
[116] Doris Kearns Goodwin, *Team of Rivals* 588 (2005).
[117] *Id.* at 732.
[118] Richard White, *The Republic for Which It Stands: The United States during Reconstruction and the Gilded Age, 1865-1896*, 2 (2017).
[119] Theodore Roosevelt Association, "The Author," http://www.theodoreroosevelt.org/site/c.elKSIdOWIiJ8H/b.8344387/k.2C4D/The_Author.htm
[120] Brandon Rottinghaus & Justin Vaughn, "New ranking of U.S. presidents puts Lincoln at No. 1, Obama at 18; Kennedy judged most overrated," February 16, 2015, https://www.washingtonpost.com/news/monkey-cage/wp/2015/02/16/new-ranking-of-u-s-presidents-puts-lincoln-1-obama-18-kennedy-judged-most-over-rated/?utm_term=.3e4686da5a6c.
[121]Theodore Roosevelt, "Man in the Arena," April 23, 1910, Theodore Roosevelt Association, http://www.theodoreroosevelt.org/site/c.elKSIdOWIiJ8H/b.9274065/k.8422/Man_in_the_Arena.htm.
[122] Sandel, *supra* note 33, at 219.
[123] U.S. Department of Education, "120 Years of American Education: A Statistical Portrait," January 1993, https://nces.ed.gov/pubs93/93442.pdf.
[124] Mark Twain, *The Gilded Age: A Tale of Today* 98-100 (1904).
[125] Boorstin, *supra* note 75, at 107-11.
[126] Harry Clemons, "The Connecticut Magazine: An Illustrated Monthly," Volume 11 (1907)
[127] Leach, *supra* note 112, at 19.
[128] Boorstin, *supra* note 75, at 146.
[129] Walter Lippmann, *Drift and Mastery* 92, 119 (1914).
[130] Vintage Ad Browser, "Coke/ Coca-Cola Advertisements of the 1920s," http://www.vintageadbrowser.com/coke-ads-1920s; Boorstin, *supra* note 75, at 147.
[131] Boorstin, *supra* note 75, at 145.
[132] Edward L. Bernays, *Public Relations*, Chapter 10 (1952).
[133] Edward L. Bernays, *Propaganda*, 47-52 (1928).
[134] Dennis W. Johnson, *Democracy for Hire: A History of American Political Consulting* 17 (2017).
[135] Bernays, *supra* note 133 at 94.

[136] William E. Geist, "Selling Soap to Children and Hairnets to Women," NYT Books, March 27, 1985, https://archive.nytimes.com/www.nytimes.com/books/98/08/16/specials/bernays-selling.html.
[137] Anne Marie O'Keefe & Richard W. Pollay, *Deadly Targeting of Women in Promoting Cigarettes*, January/April 1996, http://www.columbia.edu/itc/hs/pubhealth/p9740/readings/okeefe.pdf.
[138] Bill Moyers, "The Image Makers," April 14, 1983, https://billmoyers.com/content/image-makers/.
[139] O'Keefe, *supra* note 137.
[140] Allan Brandt, *The Cigarette Century: The Rise, Fall, and Deadly Persistence of the Product That Defined America*, 84-85 (2009).
[141] Scott M. Cutlip, *The Unseen Power: Public Relations: A History*, 185 (2016).
[142] Adolf Hitler, *Mein Kampf* vol. I, ch. X translated into English by James Murphy (2002).
[143] Dennis W. Johnson, *Routledge Handbook of Political Management*, 314 n.3 (2010).
[144] Stevenson, *supra* note 1 at 94-95.
[145] Tom Herbert, "Facebook investor says the website has become like Nazi propaganda," Metro UK, Nov. 11, 2017, https://metro.co.uk/2017/11/11/facebook-investor-says-the-website-has-become-like-nazi-propaganda-7071738/?ito=cbshare?ito=cbshare; Noah Kulwin, "You Have a Persuasion Engine Unlike Any Created in History," http://nymag.com/selectall/2018/04/roger-mcnamee-early-facebook-investor-interview.html.
[146] Jane Mayer, *Dark Money* 27-33 (2016).
[147] Edwin Black, "IBM and the Holocaust," NYT Books, October 2000, https://archive.nytimes.com/www.nytimes.com/books/first/b/black-ibm.html?mcubz=1.
[148] Leach, *supra* note 112, at 11.
[149] Theodore Roosevelt, *The New Nationalism* 244 (1910); Sandel, *supra* note 33 at 217, 221.
[150] Sandel, *supra* note 33, at 216.
[151] Sandel, *supra* note 33, at 221, 223.
[152] Calvin Coolidge, "Address to the American Society of Newspaper Editors, Washington, D.C.," January 17, 1925, The American Presidency Project, http://www.presidency.ucsb.edu/ws/?pid=24180.
[153] Sandel, *supra* note 33, at 232.
[154] Jeffrey Rosen, *Louis D. Brandeis: American Prophet* 76 (2016).
[155] Sandel, *supra* note 33, at 240-42.

[156] *Id.* at 242 (citing Mark J. Green, *The Monopoly Makers: Ralph Nader's Study Group Report on Regulation and Competition*).
[157]Adam Smith, *A Theory of Moral Sentiments*, Part VII, Chap iii, 157- 158 (1759).
[158] Jessica Weisberg, "What Dale Carnegie's 'How to Win Friends and Influence People' Can Teach the Modern Worker," The New Yorker, April 2, 2018, https://www.newyorker.com/books/page-turner/what-dale-carnegies-how-to-win-friends-and-influence-people-can-teach-the-modern-worker.
[159] Paul Y. Anderson, "Sad Death of a Hero," The American Mercury, March 1936, https://www.unz.com/print/AmMercury-1936mar-00293/.
[160] Boorstin, *supra* note 75, at 467-68; Dwight Garner, "Classic Advice: Please, Leave Well Enough Alone," NYT Books, October 5, 2011, https://www.nytimes.com/2011/10/05/books/books-of-the-times-classic-advice-please-leave-well-enough-alone.html.
[161] Dale Carnegie, *How to Win Friends and Influence People* 17 (1936).
[162] *Id.* at 5.
[163] Gail Thain Parker, "How to Win Friends and Influence People: Dale Carnegie and the Problem of Sincerity," American Quarterly, Vol. 29, No. 5, Winter 1977,
https://www.jstor.org/stable/pdf/2712571.pdf?refreqid=excelsior%3A950931d0ab29bcc6d768d4b0fbf93e33.
[164] Weisberg, *supra* note 157.
[165] Arthur Miller, *Death of a Salesman* Act 1 (1949).
[166] Richard Huber, *The Idea of American Success* 454-55 (1971)
[167] Isaacson, *supra* note 4, 89-90.
[168] John Swansburg, "The Self-Made Man," Slate, Sept 29, 2014,
http://www.slate.com/articles/news_and_politics/history/2014/09/the_self_made_man_history_of_a_myth_from_ben_franklin_to_andrew_carnegie.html.
[169] Ralph Waldo Emerson, "The American Scholar," August 31, 1837, Emerson Central, https://emersoncentral.com/texts/nature-addresses-lectures/addresses/the-american-scholar/.
[170] Carnegie, *supra* note 161 at 41.
[171] Dr. Martin Luther King, Jr., "Letter from Birmingham Jail," August 1963,
https://web.cn.edu/kwheeler/documents/Letter_Birmingham_Jail.pdf.
[172] Ronald W. Evans, *This Happened in America: Harold Rugg and the Censure of Social Studies* xvi (2007).
[173] Harold O. Rugg, ed., *The Social Studies in the Elementary and Secondary School*, 1-7 (1923).

[174] Liora Bresler, et. al, *Fifty Modern Thinkers on Education: From Piaget to the Present Day* 12 -13 (2002).
[175] Harold O. Rugg, *Problems of American Culture*, 604 (1931).
[176] Evans, *supra* note 172 at xiv.
[177] Inger L. Stole, *Advertising on Trial: Consumer Activism and Corporate Public Relations in the 1930s*, 179 (2006)
[178] Richard Crawford, "Textbook Author was Accused as Un-American," *San-Diego Times-Tribune*, February 17, 2011, http://www.sandiegoyesterday.com/wp-content/uploads/2011/03/Textbook-Controversy.pdf.
[179] Evans, *supra* note 172 at xv.
[180] Stole, *supra* note 177 at 179.
[181] Rippa, S. Alexander. "The Textbook Controversy and the Free Enterprise Campaign, 1940-1941." *History of Education Journal*, vol. 9, no. 3, 1958, pp. 49–58. *JSTOR*, JSTOR, www.jstor.org/stable/3692590.
[182] Evans, *supra* note 171 at xv.
[183] Kevin Krause, *One Nation Under God: How Corporate America Invented Christian America* 3-4 (2015)
[184]Rippa, *supra* note 181.
[185] Crawford, *supra* note 178.
[186]Rippa, *supra* note 181.
[187] Ronald W. Evans, "The Rugg Prototype for a Democratic Education," International Journal of Social Education Volume 22, Number 2, Fall 2007-2008, Pg 101-135, https://files.eric.ed.gov/fulltext/EJ818478.pdf.
[188] Oswald Spengler, *The Decline of the West* 106 (1928).
[189] Walter Lippmann, *The Phantom Public* 116 (1925).
[190] John P. Diggins, *The Promise of Pragmatism: Modernism and the Crisis of Knowledge and Authority* 300 (1995).
[191] Alan Brinkley, "The Legacy of John F. Kennedy," The Atlantic, JFK Issue, https://www.theatlantic.com/magazine/archive/2013/08/the-legacy-of-john-f-kennedy/309499/.
[192] Theodore C. Sorensen, *Let the Word Go Forth: The Speeches, Statements, and Writings of John F. Kennedy 1947 to 1963*, 210-11 (1988).
[193] Robert Dallek, *An Unfinished Life* 393 (2003).
[194] Sorensen, *supra* note 192 at 178.
[195] *Id*. at 60-61.
[196] Dallek, *supra* note 193 at 338-40.
[197] Brinkley, *supra* note 191.
[198] *Id*.
[199] Hunter S. Thompson, *Fear and Loathing on the Campaign Trial '72* 123-24 (1973).

[200] Jimmy Carter, "The Malaise Speech," July 15, 1979, The American Presidency Project, http://www.presidency.ucsb.edu/ws/?pid=32596.
[201] Will Bunch, *Tear Down this Myth*, 34-35 (2009).
[202] Moyers, *supra* note 138.
[203] Thomas W. Evans, *The Education of Ronald Reagan: The General Electric Years and the Untold Story of His Conversion to Conservatism* 43 (2006).
[204] Christopher Simpson, *The Splendid Blond Beast: Money, Law, and Genocide in the Twentieth Century* Chapter 18 (2017).
[205] Bunch, *supra* note 201 at 36-37.
[206] Evans, *supra* note 203 at 38; Bernays, *supra* note 133 at 156.
[207] Jacob Weisburg, "The Road to Reagandom," Slate, January 8, 2016, http://www.slate.com/articles/news_and_politics/politics/2016/01/ronald_reagan_s_conservative_conversion_as_spokesman_for_general_electric.html.
[208] Evans, *supra* note 203 at 38; Lou Cannon, "Ronald Reagan: Life Before the Presidency," Miller Center, https://millercenter.org/president/reagan/life-before-the-presidency
[209] Bunch, *supra* note 201 at 39.
[210] *Id.*
[211] Bill Boyarsky, *The Rise of Ronald Reagan* 230 (1968).
[212] Josh Zeitz, "How Trump Is Recycling Nixon's 'Law and Order' Playbook," Politico, July 18, 2016, https://www.politico.com/magazine/story/2016/07/donald-trump-law-and-order-richard-nixon-crime-race-214066.
[213] Jimmy Carter, "Welfare Reform Message to Congress," August 6, 1977, The American Presidency Project, http://www.presidency.ucsb.edu/ws/?pid=7942.
[214] Peter Edelman, *Welfare and the Politics of Race: Same Tune, New Lyrics*, 11 Geo. J. on Poverty L. & Pol'y 389, 395 (2004)
[215] Congressional Record, "Proceedings and Debates of the 104th Congress, First Session," Vol. 141, No. 55, https://www.govinfo.gov/content/pkg/CREC-1995-03-24/pdf/CREC-1995-03-24.pdf
[216] Peter Edelman, "The Worst Thing Bill Clinton has Done," The Atlantic, March 1997, https://www.theatlantic.com/magazine/archive/1997/03/the-worst-thing-bill-clinton-has-done/376797/.
[217] Glenn Kessler, "When did McConnell say he wanted to make Obama a 'one-term president'?," *Washington Post*, Sept. 25, 2012, https://www.washingtonpost.com/blogs/fact-checker/post/when-did-mcconnell-say-he-wanted-to-make-obama-a-one-term-

president/2012/09/24/79fd5cd8-0696-11e2-afff-d6c7f20a83bf_blog.html?utm_term=.1ba1c06ecce6.
[218] Lee Lescaze, "Reagan Still Sure Some in New Deal Espoused Fascism," *Washington Post*, Dec. 24, 1981, https://www.washingtonpost.com/archive/politics/1981/12/24/reagan-still-sure-some-in-new-deal-espoused-fascism/928d80c5-3211-4217-85df-d775e1566c41/?utm_term=.0e17f17ad431.
[219] "The Things Reagan Gets Away With," *Washington Post*, December 27, 1981, https://www.washingtonpost.com/archive/opinions/1981/12/27/the-things-reagan-gets-away-with/69c14b2f-1d4e-43ff-a3f9-1dd9f3acc7ba/?utm_term=.f2b190e783f4.
[220] George Orwell, *Politics and the English Language* 19 (1946).
[221] Cannon, *supra* note 208.
[222] David Corn, "Nixon on Tape: Reagan Was 'Shallow' and of 'Limited Mental Capacity,'" Mother Jones, Nov. 16, 2007, https://www.motherjones.com/politics/2007/11/nixon-tape-reagan-was-shallow-and-limited-mental-capacity/
[223] Bunch, *supra* note 201 at 43.
[224] Robert Bray, *Reading with Lincoln* 162 (2010).
[225] Ronald Reagan, *American Life* 231 (1990).
[226] Bunch, *supra* note 201 at 54-55, 60-61.
[227] Tom Shales, "Reagan's Mighty Valedictory," *Washington Post*, August 16, 1998, https://www.washingtonpost.com/archive/lifestyle/1988/08/16/reagans-mighty-valedictory/5a74f2ac-72bc-41bf-94d9-da9dd74ea861/?utm_term=.5945744a3205.
[228] Michael Beschloss, "The Ad That Helped Reagan Sell Good Times to an Uncertain Nation," *New York Times*, May 8, 2016, https://www.nytimes.com/2016/05/08/business/the-ad-that-helped-reagan-sell-good-times-to-an-uncertain-nation.html.
[229] *Id.*
[230] Joshua Holland, "The First Iraq War Was Also Sold to the Public Based on a Pack of Lies," Billmoyers.com, June 27, 2014, https://billmoyers.com/2014/06/27/the-first-iraq-war-was-also-sold-to-the-public-based-on-a-pack-of-lies/; Robert Sapolsky, *Behave: The Biology of Humans at our Best and at our Worst* 632-33 (2017).
[231] H&K Canada, "Lessons from the master," August 15, 2013, http://hkstrategies.ca/canada/en-ca/lessons-from-the-master/.
[232] "The Clinton Years: Interview with George Stephanopoulos by Chris Burg," PBS, July 2000,

https://www.pbs.org/wgbh/pages/frontline/shows/clinton/interviews/stephanopoulos.html.

[233] REVIEW: of Behind the Oval Office Winning the Presidency in the Nineties. By Dick Morris (James B. Stewart, NY Times Book Review).

[234] *Id.*; Adam Curtis, "A Century of the Self," BBC TV, 2002, transcript available at http://pialogue.info/books/Century-of-the-Self.php.

[235] Tom Englehardt, "Catapulting the Propaganda: The President, Cindy Sheehan, and How Words Die," Mother Jones, Aug. 29, 20005, https://www.motherjones.com/politics/2005/08/catapulting-propaganda/.

[236] D.J. Flynn, et al., "The Nature and Origins of Misperceptions: Understanding False and Unsupported Beliefs about Politics," European Research Council, https://www.dartmouth.edu/~nyhan/nature-origins-misperceptions.pdf.

[237] *Id.* at 3.

[238] *Id.*

[239] Leon Festinger, et al., *When Prophecy Fails* 3 (1957).

[240] Cass R. Sustein, *#Republic: Divided Democracy in the Age of Social Media* 93-94 (2018).

[241] *Id.* at 94.

[242] Aldous Huxley, *Brave New World* 234-35 (1932).

[243] Jonas T. Kaplan, et al., "Neural correlates of maintaining one's political beliefs in the face of counterevidence," Scientific Reports (2016), https://www.nature.com/articles/srep39589

[244] "Hard-wired: The brain's circuitry for political belief," Science Daily, Dec. 23, 2016, https://www.sciencedaily.com/releases/2016/12/161223115757.htm.

[245] Julie Beck, "This Article Won't Change Your Mind," The Atlantic, Mar. 13, 2017, https://www.theatlantic.com/science/archive/2017/03/this-article-wont-change-your-mind/519093/.

[246] Edward Bernays, *Crystallizing Public Opinion* 122 (1923).

[247] Beck, *supra* note 245.

[248] Sustein, *supra* note 240. at 100.

[249] Timothy Noah, *The Great Divergence* 1 (2012)

[250] *Id.* at 176.

[251] Thomas Piketty, et al., "Distributional National Accounts: Methods and Estimates for the United States," September 25, 2017, http://gabriel-zucman.eu/files/PSZ2017.pdf; David Leonhardt, "Our Broken Economy, in One Simple Chart," *New York Times*, Aug. 7, 2017, https://www.nytimes.com/interactive/2017/08/07/opinion/leonhardt-income-inequality.html.

---

[252] Sam-Adler Bell, "The Remnant and the Restless Crowd, Commonwealth Magazine, Aug. 1, 2018, https://www.commonwealmagazine.org/remnant-and-restless-crowd.
[253] Joy Crane and Matt Stieb, New York Magazine, 26-27 (August 6-19 2019); Maggie Astor, "Want to Be Happy? Try Moving to Finland," *New York Times*, Mar. 14, 2018, https://www.nytimes.com/2018/03/14/world/europe/worlds-happiest-countries.html.
[254] Astor, *supra* note 253.
[255] Bernays, *supra* note 133 at 156.
[256] William Lee Miller, *President Lincoln: The Duty of a Statesman* 46 (2009)
[257] Dr. Martin Luther King, Jr., "Where Do We Go From Here?", August 16, 1967, the Martin Luther King, Jr. Papers Project, https://kinginstitute.stanford.edu/king-papers/documents/where-do-we-go-here-address-delivered-eleventh-annual-sclc-convention.
[258] Frederick Schauer, *Thinking Like a Lawyer* 105 (2009).
[259] Brian Mahoney, "Pence on Labor," Politico, July 15, 2016, https://www.politico.com/tipsheets/morning-shift/2016/07/pence-on-labor-four-house-dems-attack-ot-rule-the-future-of-the-persuader-rule-215354.
[260] Jane Mayer, "The Danger of President Pence," The New Yorker, October 23, 2017, https://www.newyorker.com/magazine/2017/10/23/the-danger-of-president-pence.
[261]Browne, M. Neil; Rex, Justin; and Herrera, David L., "Potential Tension Between a 'Free Marketplace of Ideas' and the Fundamental Purpose of Free Speech" (2012). Economics Faculty Publications.
[262] *Id.*
[263] Theodore Roosevelt, "Fifth Annual Message," Dec. 5, 1905, The American Presidency Project, http://www.presidency.ucsb.edu/ws/index.php?pid=29546.
[264] Dr. Martin Luther King, Jr., "Facing the Challenge of a New Age," Dec. 3, 1956, The Martin Luther King Papers Project, https://kinginstitute.stanford.edu/king-papers/documents/facing-challenge-new-age-address-delivered-first-annual-institute-nonviolence#ftnref19.
[265] Jane Addams, "the subjective necessity for social settlements," 1892, http://www.infed.org/archives/e-texts/addams6.htm/
[266] Frederick Douglass, "Fifth of July Speech," July 5, 1852, The Frederick Douglass Project, https://rbscp.lib.rochester.edu/2945.

[267] Dr. Martin Luther King, Jr., *Why We Can't Wait*, reprinted in James M. Washington, "A Testament of Hope: The Essential Writings and Speeches of Martin Luther King Jr.," 525 (1986).
[268] Susan B. Anthony, "On Women's Right to Vote," 1873, http://www.historyplace.com/speeches/anthony.htm.
[269] Barbara Jordan, "1976 Democratic National Convention Keynote Address," July 12, 1976, http://www.americanrhetoric.com/speeches/barbarajordan1976dnc.html.
[270] Eleanor Roosevelt, "The Struggle for Human Rights," Sept. 28, 1948, http://www.americanrhetoric.com/speeches/eleanorroosevelt.htm.
[271] Deloitte, "2018 Deloitte Millennial Survey," 13 https://www2.deloitte.com/content/dam/Deloitte/global/Documents/About-Deloitte/gx-2018-millennial-survey-report.pdf
[272] Henry David Thoreau, *Walden,* 1854, http://www.literaturepage.com/read/walden-39.html.
[273] John Adams, "Letter to H. Niles," Feb. 13, 1818, http://teachingamericanhistory.org/library/document/john-adams-to-h-niles/.
[274] Selected Dialogues of Plato; Plato, *Apology* 29 d-e (Benjamin Jowett Trans.) (2001)
[275] Plato, *Meno,* (Benjamin Jowett Trans.), http://classics.mit.edu/Plato/meno.html.
[276] Dr. Martin Luther King, Jr., *Where Do We Go From Here*, reprinted in James M. Washington, "A Testament of Hope: The Essential Writings and Speeches of Martin Luther King Jr.," 557 (1986).
[277] *Id.* at 565.
[278] Lyndon B. Johnson, "The American Promise," March 15, 1965, LBJ Presidential Library, http://www.lbjlibrary.org/lyndon-baines-johnson/speeches-films/president-johnsons-special-message-to-the-congress-the-american-promise.
[279] "From Thomas Jefferson to William Charles Jarvis, 28 September 1820," Founders Online, National Archives, last modified June 13, 2018, http://founders.archives.gov/documents/Jefferson/98-01-02-1540.
[280] John Adams, "Thoughts on Government," Apr. 1776 Papers 4:86-93, http://www.constitution.org/jadams/thoughts.htm; John Adams, *A Defense of the Constitutions of Government*, Chapter 18 (1787).
[281] "UD Library discovers Thomas Jefferson letter," UDaily, Dec. 3, 2009, http://www1.udel.edu/udaily/2010/dec/jefferson120309.html
[282] "The College Seal," Dickinson College, http://www.dickinson.edu/info/20085/marketing_and_communications/1473/college_seal.

---

[283] Letter to Abigail Adams (29 October 1775), published Letters of John Adams, Addressed to His Wife, Vol. 1 (1841), ed. Charles Francis Adams, p. 72.
[284] Gordon S. Wood, *The Creation of the American Republic, 1776-1787* 53-65 (1969).
[285] "The Writings of Thomas Paine," Vol. I (1774-1779), http://oll.libertyfund.org/quote/381.
[286] Dr. Martin Luther King, Jr., "Beyond Vietnam," April 4, 1967, the Martin Luther King, Jr. Papers Project, https://kinginstitute.stanford.edu/encyclopedia/beyond-vietnam.

Made in the USA
Middletown, DE
06 February 2020

84323985R00120